Piano: 2nd Time Around...

A refresher piano course for adults
by James Bastien and Jane Smisor Bastien

Piano: 2nd Time Around is designed as a basic review for an adult who is somewhat beyond the beginning stages of playing the piano—a refresher course for the student who is returning to the piano after a leave of absence.

The book may be used in private or group lessons. At the college level it may be used for students who have had piano lessons prior to college, and who are too advanced for a beginning class.

There are five main sections in the book. The student may use more than one section at a time.

Section 1: Where Are You?

is intended to be used as an initial evaluation of the student's skills.

Section 2: Once Over Lightly

is the review portion of the book providing multi-key experiences which the student may not have had previously. Included in this section are scales, chords, and pieces in various styles.

Section 3: Shape Up!

contains exercises and etudes for building and improving technic from the very first lesson.

Section 4: Attention Getters

contains pieces representing several periods of music history.

Section 5: Handy References

contains basic music theory, a list of books about music, a chronological list of composers, and other helpful information.

WP59

ISBN 0-8497-5095-4

Contents...

Section 1: Where Are You?...

Analyzing Your Background

The compositions and questions on pages 4-11 are designed to help you (and your teacher) determine what you remember from your past musical experiences. The compositions are arranged in sequence from easy to more difficult.

Look at the following pieces and choose one you assume to be your level. With or without briefly practicing the piece, play it for your teacher. Your performance and response to the questions will assist your teacher in evaluating your level. From this evaluation, material for review and study can be assigned.

Do You Know. . .

- What the key of this piece is?
- What the time signature means?
- What the tempo marking indicates?
- What the various kinds of notes and rests are and how many counts each receives?
- What the slurs indicate?
- What the dots above or below the notes indicate?
- What **mf** and **f** mean?

March

Moderato

J.W.B.

Do You Know. . .

- What the key of this piece is?
- What the flat in the key signature indicates?
- What **c** means?
- What *Allegro* means?
- What touch is required?
- What the dynamic marks (**f** **p**) indicate?
- The names of the chords, or some of them?

Rustic Dance

J.W.B.

Do You Know...

- What the key of this piece is (major or minor)?
- What each number of the time signature means?
- What *Andante con moto* means?
- What the various kinds of notes and rests are and how many beats each receives?
- What the accidentals (♭,♯,♮) indicate?
- What the slurs indicate?
- What *mp, mf, 8va, loco, dim. e rit.,* and *a tempo* mean?
- What ⌐____, and ◁, ▷, indicate and what they're called?

Reflection

J.W.B.

Do You Know...

- What the key of this piece is?
- What the sharp in the key signature indicates?
- What each of the numbers in the time signature means?
- What the tempo marking indicates?
- How to count the rhythm?
- What the slurs indicate?
- What the dynamic marks (*mf*, *f*, *p*) mean?

Minuet

J.W.B.

Do You Know. . .

- What the key of this piece is?
- What the time signature means?
- What the tempo marking indicates?
- What these notes are ♫ , ♬ , ♬ , and how they are counted?
- How to count the rhythm ♪♩♪ ?
- The names of >, ◁, ‖: :‖, *D.C. al fine* and what they indicate?

Ecossaise

Ludwig van Beethoven (1770-1827)

Do You Know...

- If this piece is in a major or minor key?
- What the key name is?
- What the time signature means?
- What the tempo marking indicates?
- What ♫♫ are called? How are they counted?
- What these terms mean: *leggiero, cresc., dim. e poco rit., a tempo, risoluto*?
- The names for >, *sfz*, 1.⌐ 2.⌐ , ⌢• , and what they indicate?
- The names of the chords, or some of them?

Arabesque

Allegro scherzando

Friedrich Burgmüller (1806-1874)

Section 2:
Once Over Lightly...
Basic Multi-key Review

All major five-finger positions and I (tonic) chords are given on these two pages. Note that the twelve keys are divided into four groups based on the keyboard position of the chord. The white boxes represent white keys; the black boxes represent black keys.

Note: These five-finger positions and chords may be played in *minor* by lowering the middle note one half-step.

Five-finger Positions and I Chords

GROUP 1 CHORDS
(C, G, F)

GROUP 2 CHORDS
(D, A, E)

GROUP 3 CHORDS
(Db, Ab, Eb)

GROUP 4 CHORDS
(Gb, Bb, B)

Gb (F#)   Bb   B

Group 1 Keys...

C Major

G Major

F Major

Group 2 Keys. . .

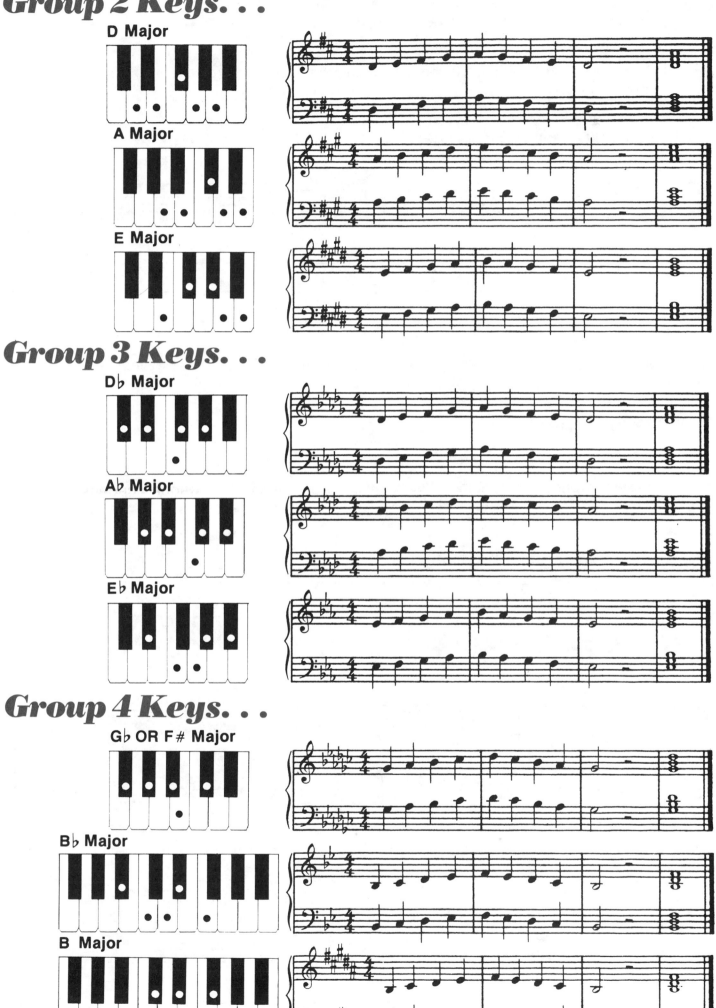

Group 3 Keys. . .

Group 4 Keys. . .

Reading in C Major. . .

Practice Numbers 1 and 2 as preparation for reading the succeeding pieces in C major. Practice hands separately at first.

1. Five-finger Position

2. Primary Chords *

Practice Numbers 3, 4, and 5 as preparation for playing more difficult music (piano literature, arrangements, pop music, etc.). Practice hands separately at first.

3. C Major Scale

4. Triads and Inversions

5. Dominant 7ths and Inversions **

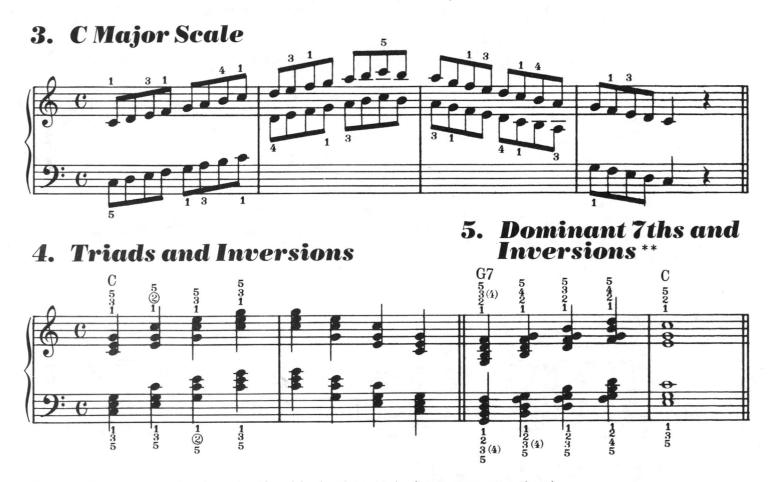

These chords may also be practiced in *broken* style (one note at a time).

For an explanation of chord symbols (C, F, G7) see page 190, and for Roman numerals (I, IV, V7) see page 188.
**Finger 3 or 4 may be used as indicated on the dominant seventh chords depending on the size of your hand.*

Waltz

Moderato

J.W.B.

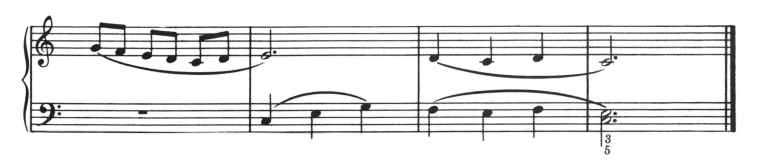

Ode to Joy

theme from the "Ninth Symphony"

Ludwig van Beethoven
arr. by J.W.B.

Moderato

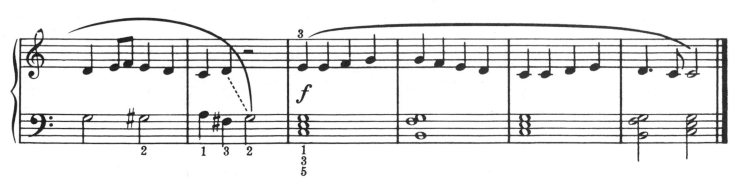

Note: When playing melody and accompaniment, the melody should always "sing" above the accompaniment. Play the accompaniment softer than the melody for the correct balance.

Song at Twilight
1.

J.W.B.

Practice the left hand *waltz bass* alone before playing with hands together. Play by "feel." Do *not* look at your hand for the chord changes.

2.

C Major Scale Etude

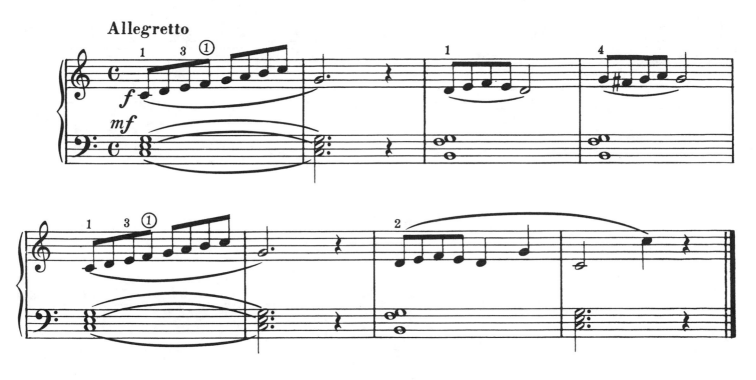

Can-Can

Jacques Offenbach (1819-1880)
arr. by J.W.B.

Etude in 6/8

Blues in C

Rock Etude

J.W.B.

Scale Etude

Dialogue

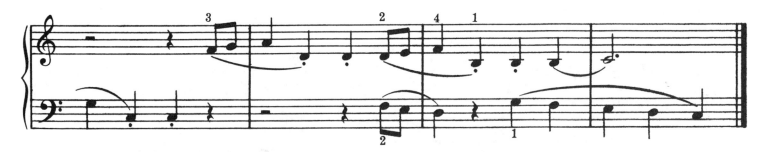

Arkansas Traveler

Folk Song

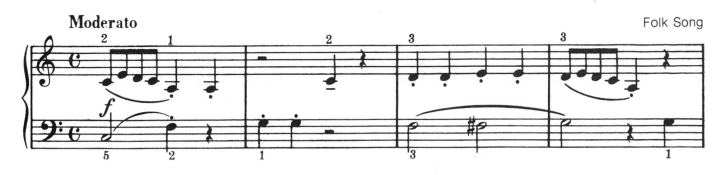

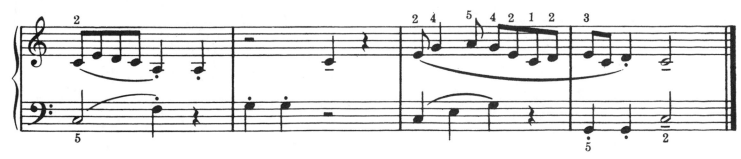

Reading in G Major...

Practice Numbers 1 and 2 as preparation for reading the succeeding pieces in G major. Practice hands separately at first.

1. Five-finger Position   ## 2. Primary Chords

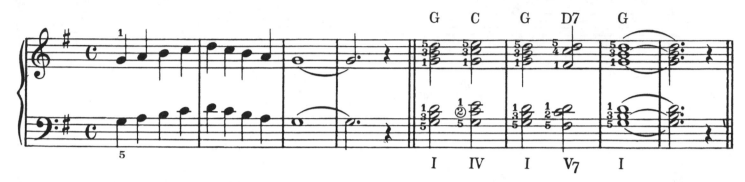

3. G Major Scale

Practice Numbers 3, 4, and 5 as preparation for playing more difficult music. Practice hands separately at first.

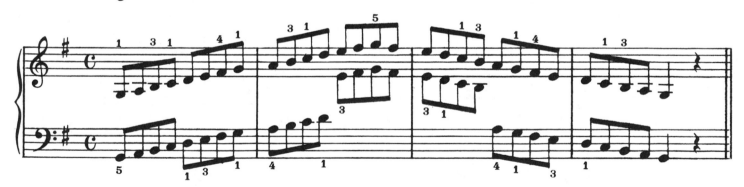

4. Triads and Inversions
(These chords may also be practiced in broken style.)

5. Dominant 7ths and Inversions

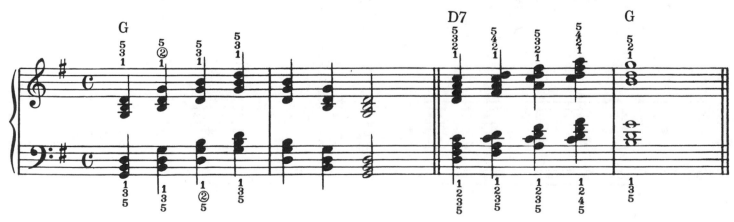

Saint Anthony Chorale

Joseph Haydn (1732-1809)
arr. by J.W.B.

Duet

J.W.B.

Rock Tune

J.S.B.

Bright rock beat

Ballad

J.W.B.

Moderato

Etude I

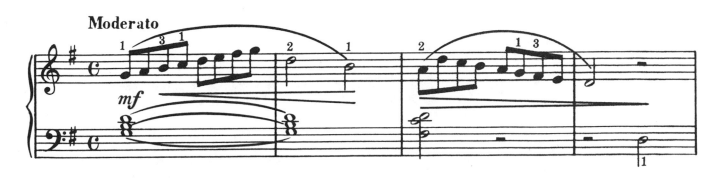

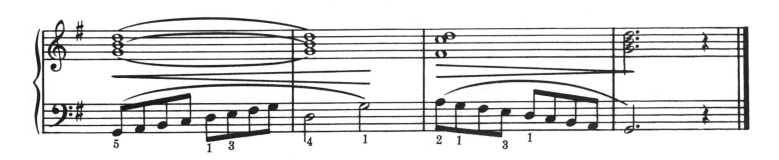

Etude II

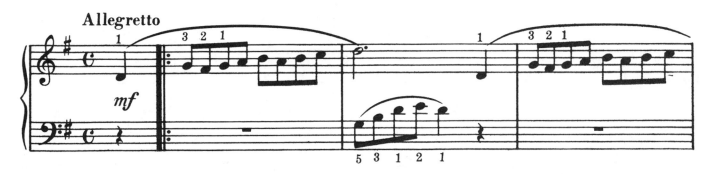

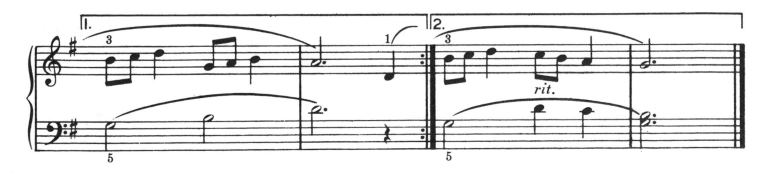

24

Practice the broken chord bass before playing this song with hands together. Play by "feel." Do *not* look at your hand for the chord changes.

Red River Valley

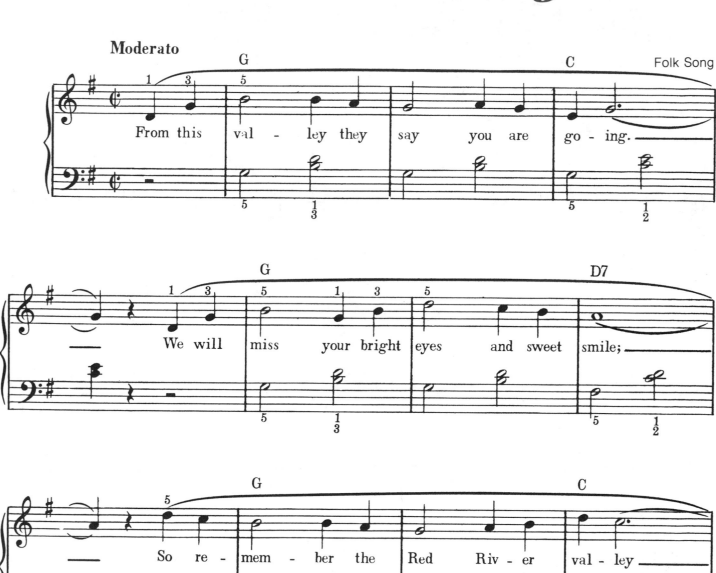

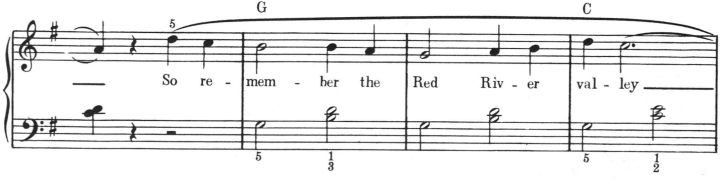

Play the melody with a singing tone and play the accompanying chords lightly. Notice that the left hand has the melody beginning in measure 9.

Lament

J.W.B.

Reading in F Major. . .

Practice Numbers 1 and 2 as preparation for reading the succeeding pieces in F major. Practice hands separately at first.

1. Five-finger Position

2. Primary Chords

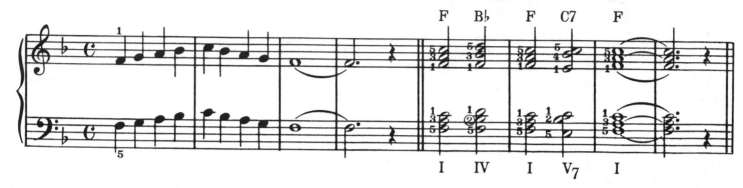

Practice Numbers 3, 4, and 5 as preparation for playing more difficult music. Practice hands separately at first. *Note:* The right hand fingering is 1 2 3 4, 1 2 3. The highest note is played with 4.

3. F Major Scale

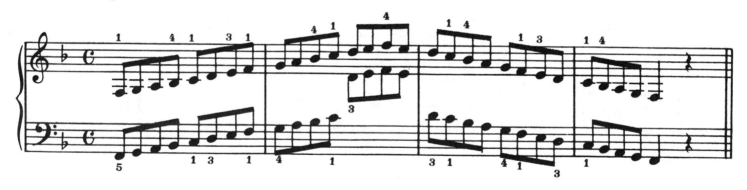

4. Triads and Inversions

5. Dominant 7ths and Inversions

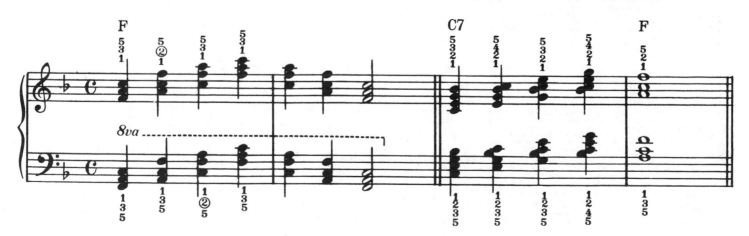

Minuet

Moderato

J.W.B.

Practice the left hand *waltz bass* alone before playing with hands together. Play by "feel." Do *not* look at your hand for the chord changes.

On Top of Old Smoky

Moderato

Folk Song

On top of Old Smok - y,_____ All cov-ered with

snow,_____ For court-in' too slow._____

I lost my true lov - er,_____

Grace Note. . .

A grace note is printed in small type. It is not counted in rhythm but is played quickly, almost together with the next note.

Scottish Bagpipes

J.W.B.

Scale Etude

Dotted Rhythm Waltz

J.W.B.

Reading in C, G, F

The following pieces provide further reading practice in the three keys learned so far: C, G, F.

To a Wild Rose

Edward MacDowell (1861-1908)
arr. by J.W.B.

Chord Symbols

In some of the previous pieces in this book, chord symbols (the chord's name) have been printed as an aid to reading. In some of the following pieces you will be asked to write in the chord symbols. The following chords are frequently used. The root of the chord (also the chord's name) is indicated in black.

Frequently used inversions:

Look through this piece before playing it. Write the chord symbols above each chord (broken or blocked). Discover the changes in hand positions. When playing, look ahead and find each new hand position quickly.

Little Rock

J.W.B.

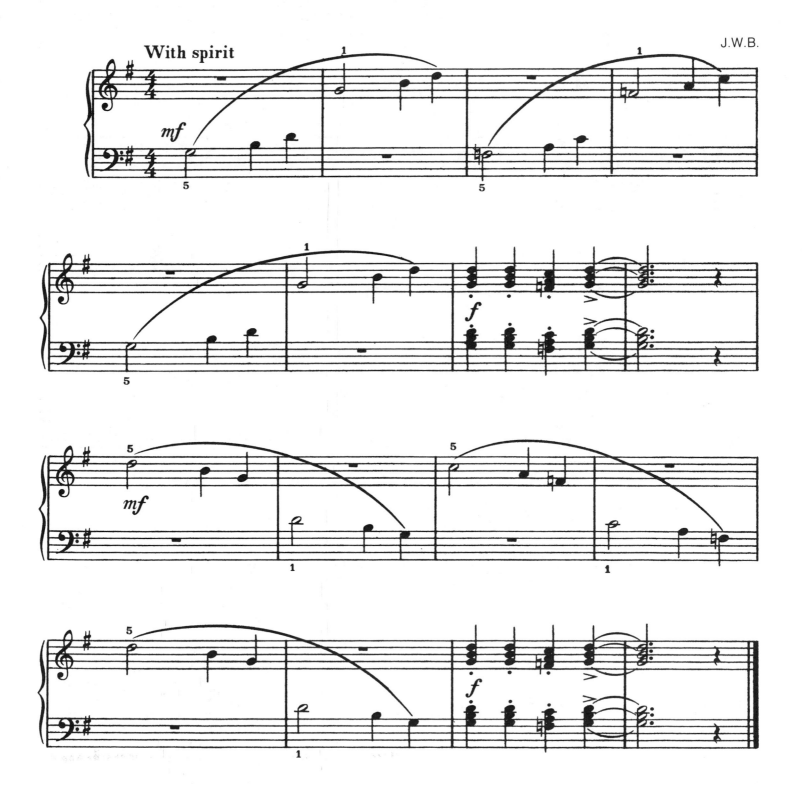

Bass Styles

The accompaniments used so far in this book have been limited to *block chords,* various *broken chords,* and the *waltz bass.* The broken chord and waltz basses are given below for review. The last one, *Alberti bass,* will be used later in this book.

Practice each style until you can play it smoothly. Play by "feel." Do *not* look at your hand for the chord changes. Play each style as written (in C major), then transpose it to G and F major.

Note: Playing music in a key other than which it is written is called *transposition.* The verb form is transpose.

Broken Chord Bass (1st style)

Broken Chord Bass (2nd style)

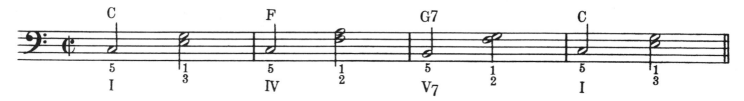

Waltz Bass

Alberti Bass

Practice the left hand chords first as block chords. Then practice the left hand broken chords as written. Play by "feel." Do *not* look at your hand for the chord changes.

Juanita

Andante

Spanish Song

Play this song again using the waltz bass shown on page 32.

The Damper Pedal

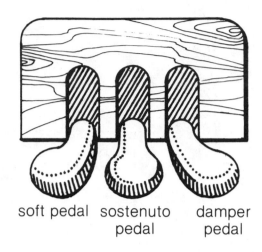

Whether your piano has two or three pedals, the one on the right is the damper pedal. When pressed, the dampers lift from the strings to allow the strings to vibrate freely. Thus, the damper pedal is used to sustain the sounds of notes. The damper pedal is the one most often used. (If you have only two pedals, the ''missing'' one is the sostenuto.)

soft pedal   sostenuto   damper
pedal   pedal

Pedal Technic

Press the damper pedal with your *right* foot. Keep your heel on the floor when you use the pedal.

press   hold   lift

Practice these exercises *before* using the pedal in the following pieces.

Pedal Etudes
1.

2.

German Folk Song

Play this song again using the waltz bass shown on page 32.

Look through this piece before playing it. Write the chord symbols above each chord (blocked or broken).

Over the Waves

Medium waltz tempo

Juventino Rosas

Practice hands separately first.

Interlude

J.S.B.

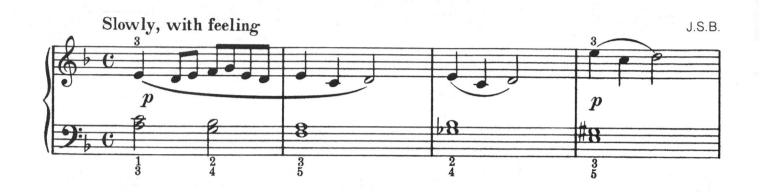

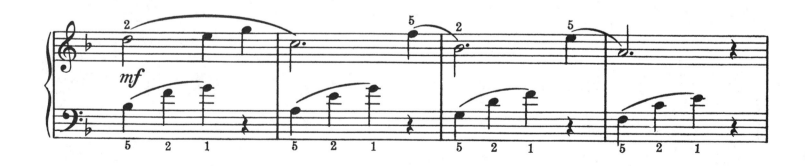

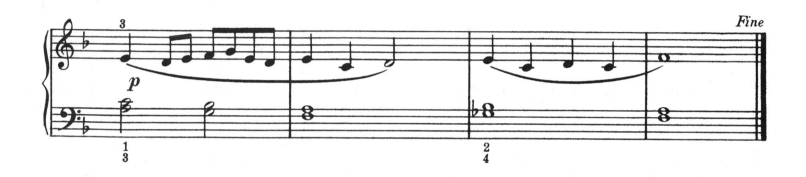

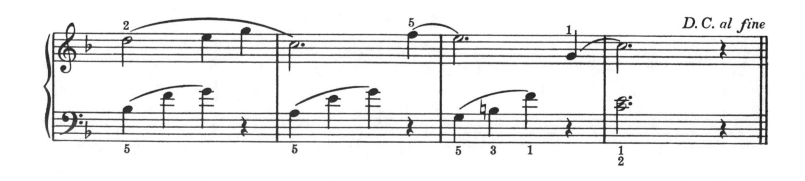

Waltz
Op. 39, No. 15

Johannes Brahms (1833-1897)
arr. by J.W.B.

Syncopation

Syncopation means to stress or accent weak beats. Often, a long note is placed on a weak beat. The syncopated rhythm pattern is short-long-short.

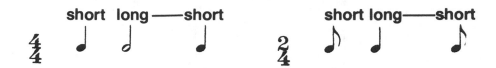

Clap and count the following rhythm. Use either of the suggested ways for counting this syncopated rhythm.

1. 1   and - 2   and   3 (and)   4 (and)
2. 8th   quar-ter   8th   quar-ter   quar-ter

Count aloud while you play the following Etudes. Use either of the suggested ways of counting. Transpose each Etude to other keys.

Syncopated Rhythm Etudes
1.

2.

Nobody Knows the Trouble I've Seen

Spiritual

Old Time Piano Rag

J.W.B.

Triplet Rhythm

A triplet eighth-note figure is equal to one quarter note:

The triplet rhythm may be counted in various ways. Clap and count the triplet rhythm in the ways given below.

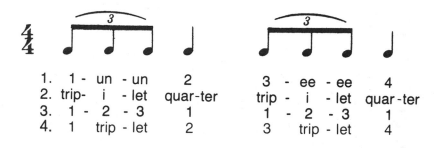

1. 1 - un - un   2   3 - ee - ee   4
2. trip- i - let   quar-ter   trip - i - let   quar-ter
3. 1 - 2 - 3   1   1 - 2 - 3   1
4. 1   trip - let   2   3   trip - let   4

Count aloud while playing the following Etudes. Use any of the ways given above for counting the triplet rhythm. Transpose each Etude to other keys.

Etudes

Stately Procession

J.W.B.

Melody

J.W.B.

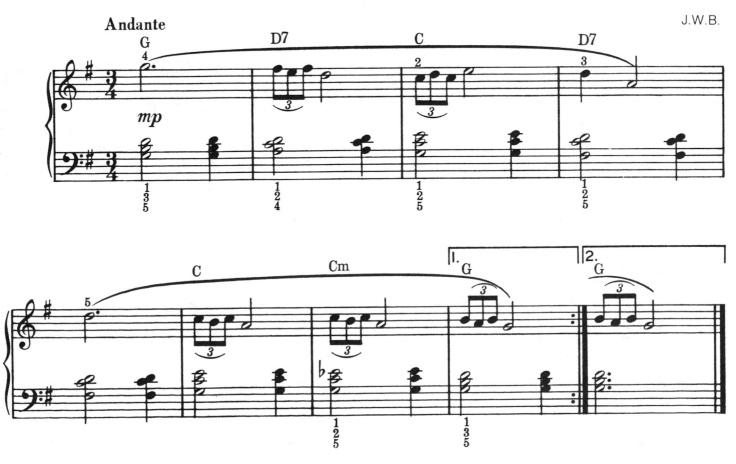

Binary Form...

This piece is in binary, or two-part form. The two parts are called Section A and Section B.

Minuet

Georg Philip Teleman (1681-1767)

March Allegro

J.S.B.

Reading in D Major

Practice Numbers 1 and 2 as preparation for reading the succeeding pieces in D Major. Practice hands separately at first.

1. Five-finger Position

2. Primary Chords

Practice Numbers 3, 4, and 5 as preparation for playing more difficult music. Practice hands separately at first.

3. D Major Scale

4. Triads and Inversions

5. Dominant 7ths and Inversions

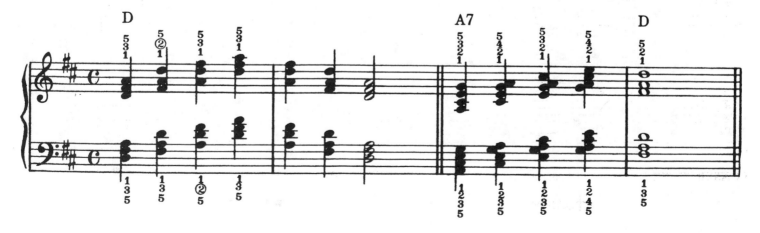

D Major Etude

Down in the Valley

Disco Beat

Bright disco beat

J.W.B.

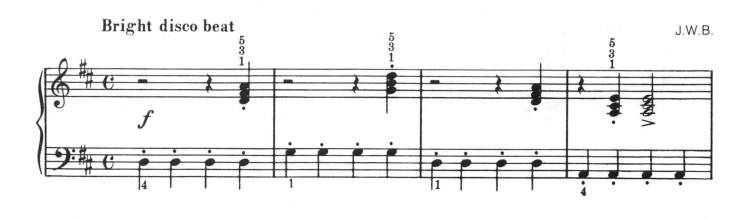

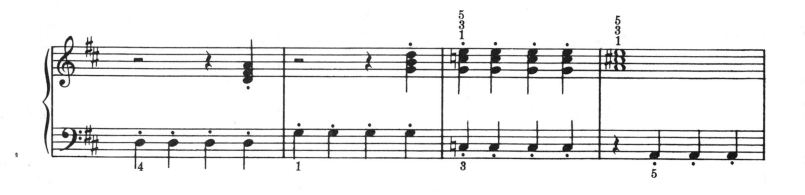

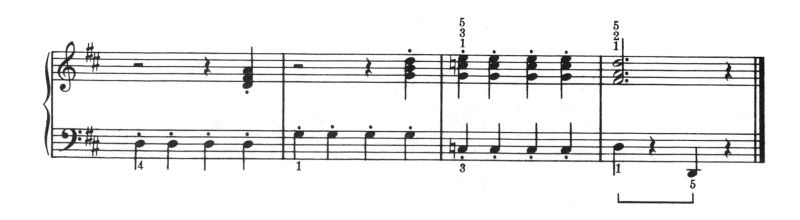

Mellow Rock

Moderate rock beat

J.S.B.

"Overlapping" Pedal Technic

The damper pedal is used to sustain and connect tones. The technic used to connect the sounds is called overlapping, or syncopated, pedaling.

Practice the following overlapping pedal Preparatory Drills with each hand playing (separately). When playing the left hand, play an octave lower than what is written.

Preparatory Drills

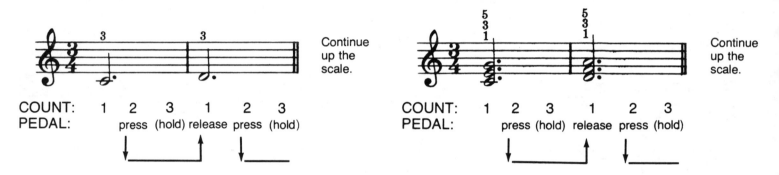

The overlapping pedal is usually shown this way:

Practice the following Pedal Study using the suggestions above.

Pedal Study

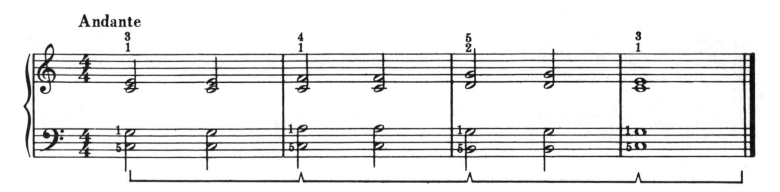

In Church

12 Bar Blues

The 12 bar blues is a chord progression pattern which is used as a basis for improvisation. In its simplest form this pattern is:

4 bars of the I chord
2 bars of the IV chord
2 bars of the I chord
1 bar of the V chord ⎱ or 2 bars of
1 bar of the IV chord ⎰ the V chord
2 bars of the I chord

Blues in C

Blue notes are flatted notes often found in blues songs. Notice the use of blue notes in Variation 1. Make up other "blue note" variations following the 12 bar blues pattern.

Variation 1

Cruel Woman

Slow blues tempo

Traditional Blues Song
arr. by J.W.B.

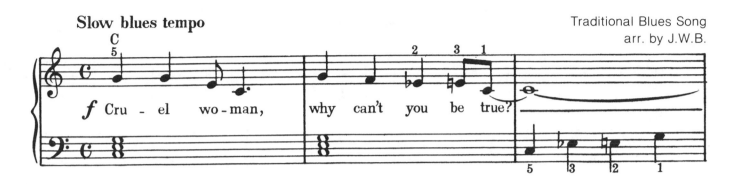

Cru - el wo - man, why can't you be true?

Cru - el wo - man, why can't you be true?

You made me love you,

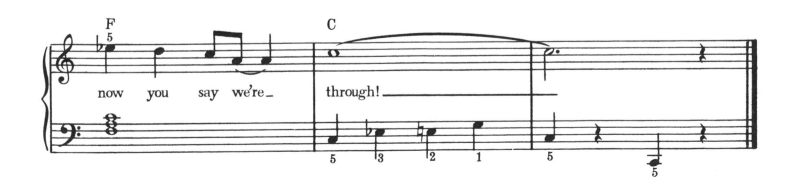

now you say we're_ through! _____

WP59

Upbeat Blues

Moderate blues tempo

J.W.B.

The 12 bar blues pattern may be altered.
In *Frankie and Johnny* the pattern is:

4 bars of the I chord
3 bars of the IV chord
1 bar of the I chord
2 bars of the V⁷ chord
2 bars of the I chord

Frankie and Johnny

Moderate blues tempo

Traditional

WP59

Major and Minor Chords

Chords are built on scale degrees. The major triad (three-note chord) built on the first tone of the major scale is formed from the first (root), third, and fifth tones of the scales. The triad is in root position when the first tone (root) is the lowest note.

To make any major chord a minor chord, lower the third tone a half step.*

These chords may be played hands separately or with hands together. Transpose each Chord Drill to other keys.

Chord Drills

1. Major-minor

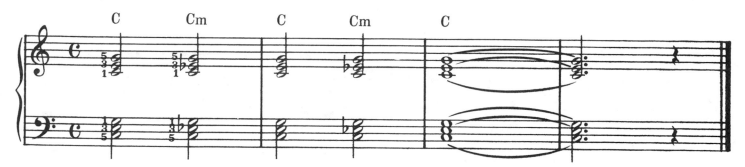

2. 1 V7 1 in Minor

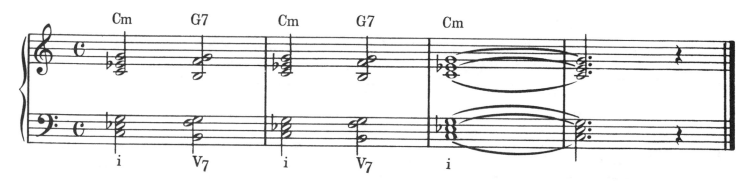

3. Primary Chords in Minor

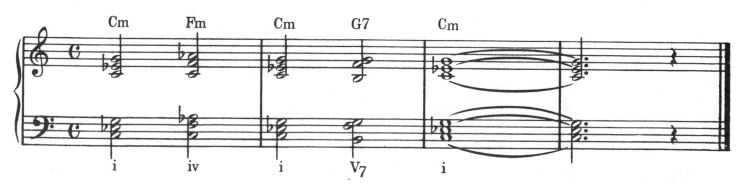

For an explanation of half step see page 188.

Name the chords used in this piece. Circle the minor chords.

Blue Mood

J.S.B.

Relative Minor Scales

There are three forms of minor scales:

1. Natural   2. Harmonic   3. Melodic

Minor scales are related to major scales because they have the same key signature (see the next page). These minor scales are referred to as relative minors.

Natural Minor

The natural minor scale uses exactly the same tones as the relative major scale, but it starts on the sixth tone of the major scale.

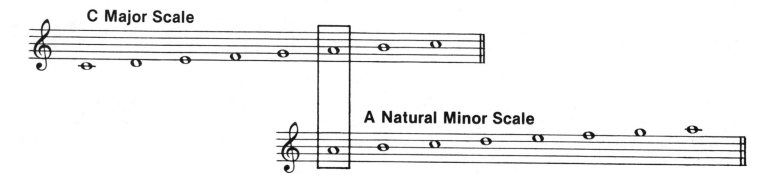

Harmonic Minor

The harmonic minor scale uses the notes of the natural minor scale, but the seventh tone (degree) is raised a half step. The raised seventh must be written in as an accidental, because it is not in the key signature.

Melodic Minor

The melodic minor scale uses the notes of the natural minor scale, but the sixth and seventh tones are raised a half step going up. The sixth and seventh tones are lowered going down.

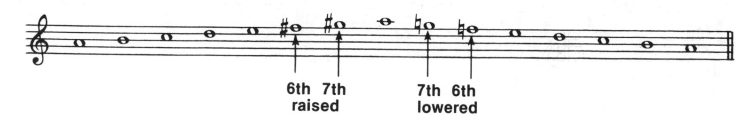

Minor Key Signatures

Major and minor scales are related by their key signatures when the key signatures are the same. Thus, A minor is relative to C major.

To tell whether a piece is in major or minor, look at the first and last notes. These are clues which help tell if it's major or minor. Also, listen to see if the piece sounds major or minor. If the piece sounds minor, you find the minor key name with this rule:

Count down three half steps from the major key name.
That is the name of the minor key.

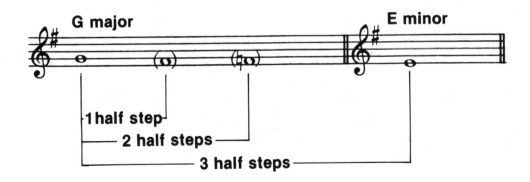

Write the minor key name on the blanks below.

Three Minor Scales

Practice each harmonic minor scale for at least a week. Play hands separately at first.

A Harmonic Minor (Relative of C Major)

D Harmonic Minor (Relative of F Major)

E Harmonic Minor (Relative of G Major)

After practicing the harmonic minor scales, play as *natural* minor scales by leaving out the written sharps in the second and third measures.

Then play as *melodic* minor scales by raising the second note of the second measure a half step and leaving out the sharp in the third measure.

Scarborough Fair

Key of _____ minor

English Folk Song

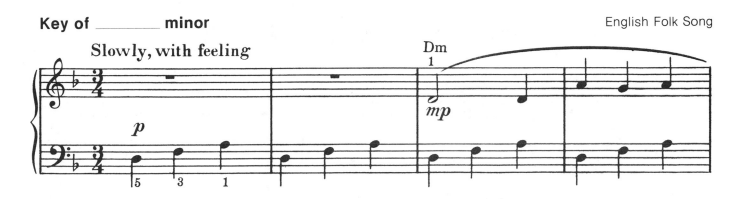

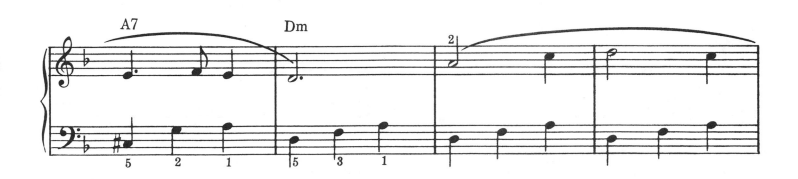

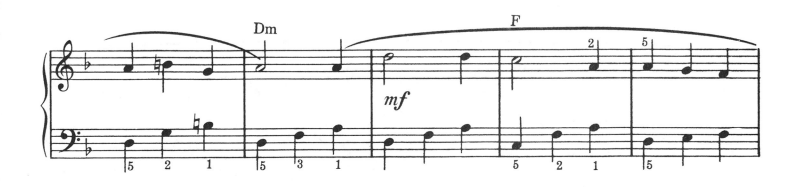

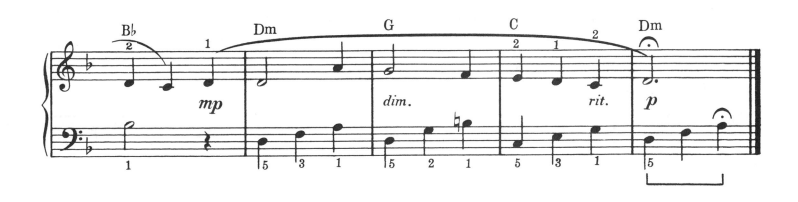

Write the chord symbols above the melody line before playing.

Greensleeves

Slowly, with feeling

English Folk Song

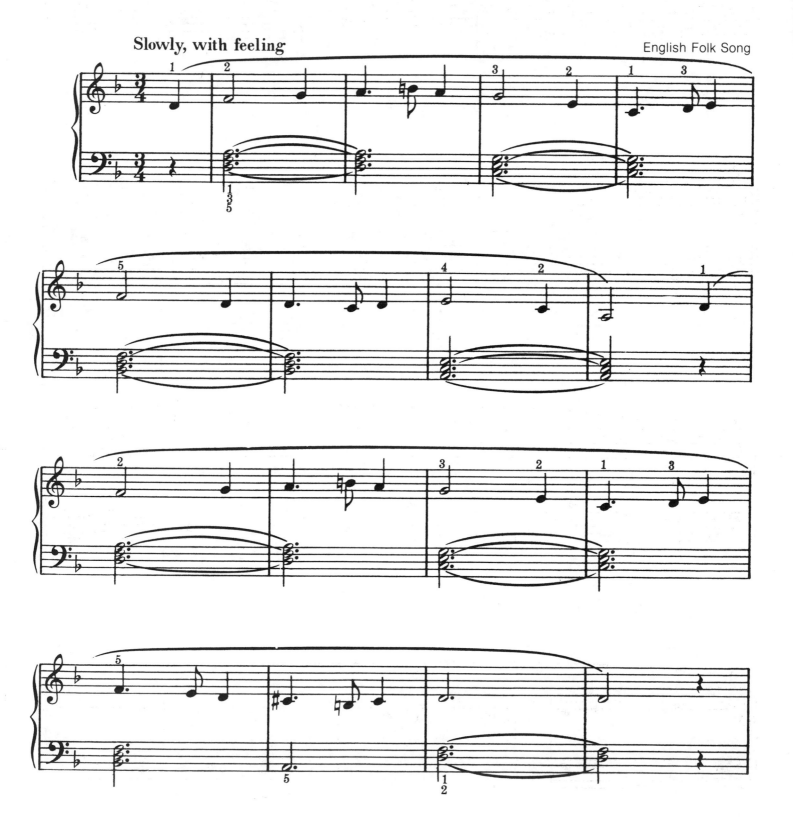

Reading in A Major

Practice Numbers 1 and 2 as preparation for reading the succeeding pieces in A major. Practice hands separately at first. Also practice these patterns in A minor.

1. Five-finger Position

2. Primary Chords

Practice Numbers 3, 4, and 5 as preparation for playing more difficult music. Practice hands separately at first.

Note: These scales and chords may also be practiced in minor keys. Refer to page 58.

3. A Major Scale

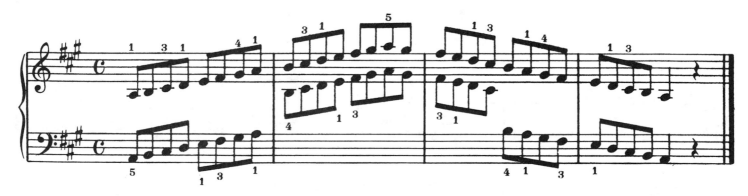

4. Triads and Inversions

5. Dominant 7ths and Inversions

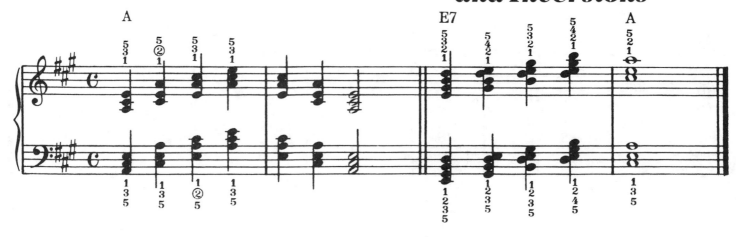

Broken Chord Etude

For He's a Jolly Good Fellow

Traditional

Theme

from "Sonata in A"

Wolfgang Amadeus Mozart (1756-1791)
arr. by J.W.B.

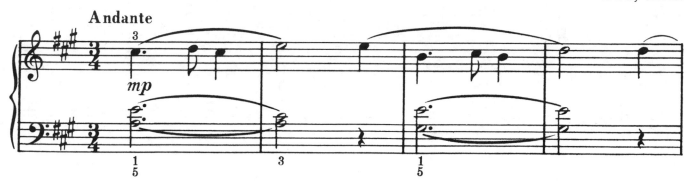

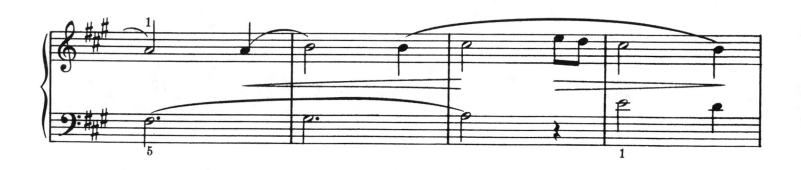

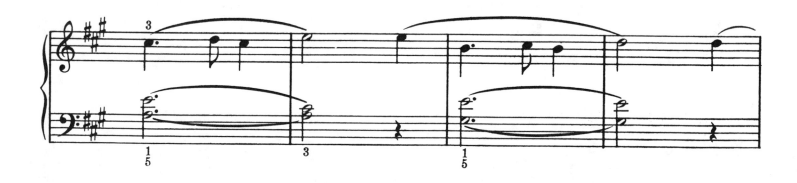

Blue Solitude

J.S.B.

Slowly

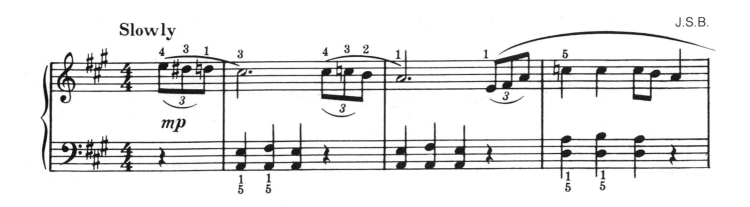

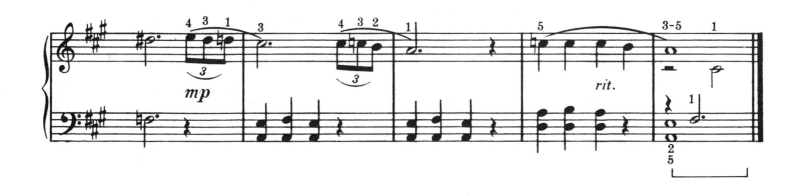

Reading in E Major

Practice Numbers 1 and 2 as preparation for reading the succeeding pieces in E major. Practice hands separately at first. Also practice these patterns in E minor.

1. Five-finger Positions

2. Primary Chords

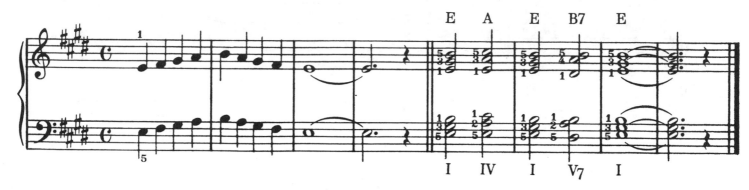

Practice Numbers 3, 4, and 5 as preparation for playing more difficult music. Practice hands separately at first.

Note: These scales and chords may also be practiced in minor keys. Refer to page 58.

3. E Major Scale

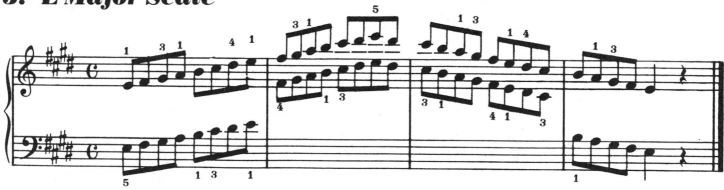

4. Triads and Inversions

5. Dominant 7ths and Inversions

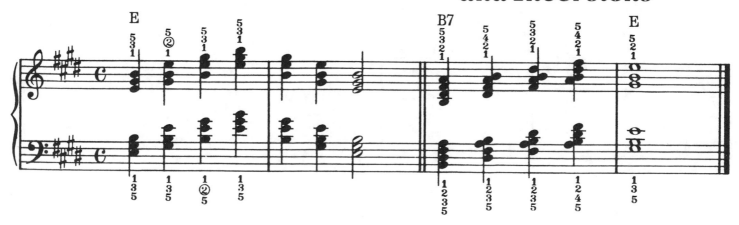

Scale Etude

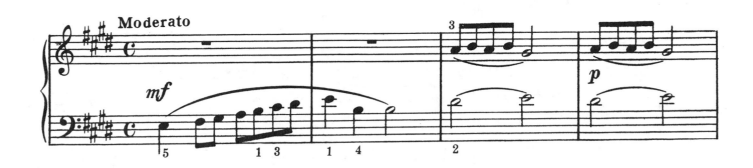

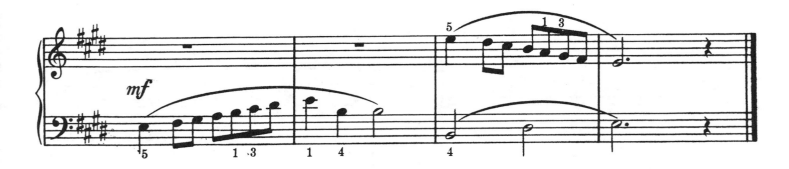

Largo

from the "New World Symphony"

Antonin Dvořák (1841-1904)
arr. by J.W.B.

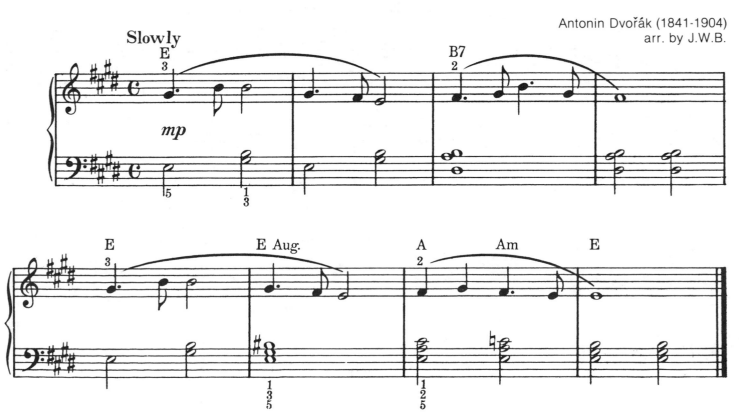

Every Night When the Sun Goes Down

Appalacian Folk Song
arr. by J.W.B.

Slowly, with feeling

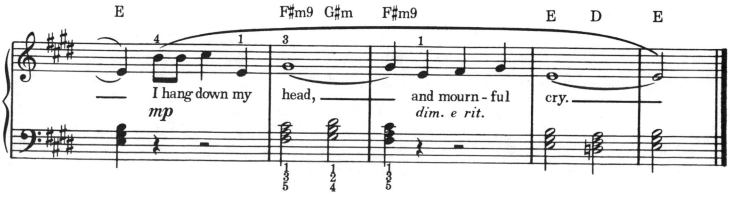

Hymn Tune

Henri F. Hemy
arr. by J.W.B.

Rockin' Little Brown Jug

Folk Song
arr. by J.S.B.

Spiritoso

The Thunderer

John Philip Sousa (1854-1932)
arr. by J.S.B.

Tempo di marcia

Triads of the Scale

A triad (three-note chord) may be built on any note of any scale.

Triads of the C major scale

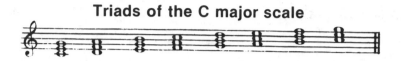

Practice the above triads forward and backward. Play first with your right hand, then with your left hand. Transpose the triads to the keys of G and F major.

March

J.W.B.

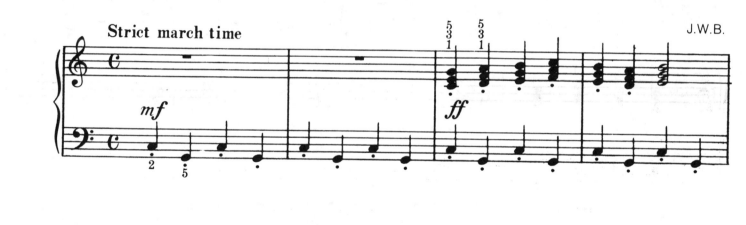

The Passing Parade

J.W.B.

Strict march time

Sea Mist

With a gentle flowing motion

J.W.B.

*15ma means to play two octaves (15 notes) higher than written.

First Inversion Triads

A first inversion triad has an interval of a third between the two bottom notes and the interval of a fourth between the top two notes. The *root* is always the *top* note of the fourth.

Examples:

   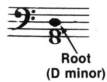

Root (C major)   Root (A minor)   Root (A major)   Root (D minor)

Find the first inversion triads in this group. Circle the root and write the name of each first inversion triad on the blank below. Play the chords.

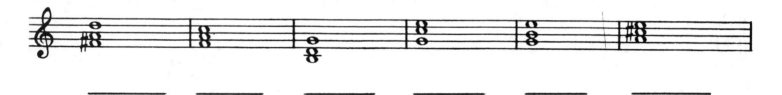

_____   _____   _____   _____   _____   _____

_____   _____   _____   _____   _____   _____

Play the first inversion triads of the C major scale. Practice hands separately. Also transpose to the keys of G and E₇

Chimes

J.W.B.

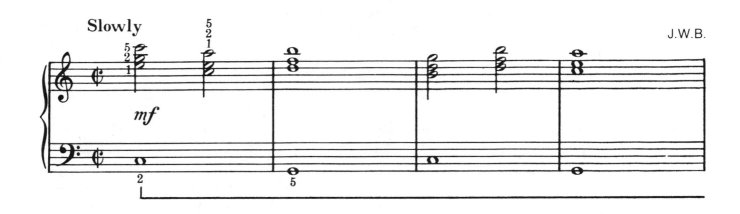

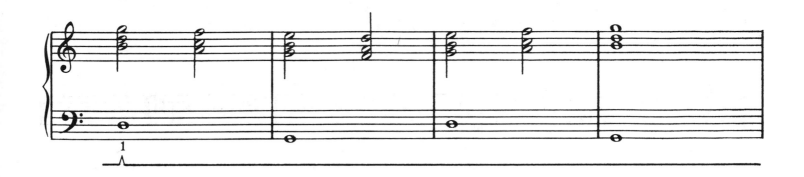

Second Inversion Triads

A second inversion triad has an interval of a third between the top two notes, and the interval of a fourth between the bottom two notes. The *root* is always the *top* note of the fourth.

3rd [ ] 4th

Examples:

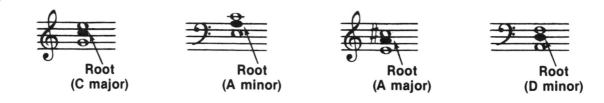

Root (C major)   Root (A minor)   Root (A major)   Root (D minor)

Find the second inversion triads in this group. Circle the root and write the name of each second inversion triad on the blank below. Play the chords.

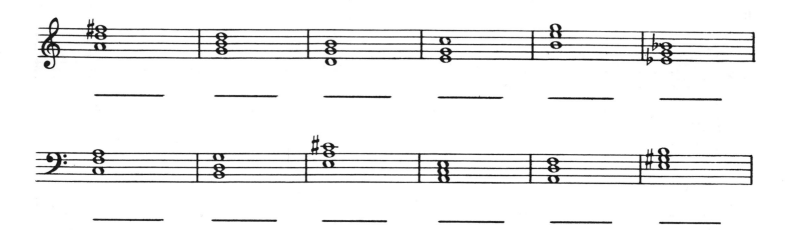

Play these second inversion triads of the C major scale. Practice hands separately. Also transpose to the keys of G and F.

Solemn Procession

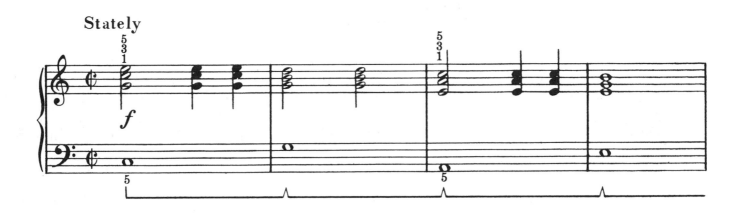

Reading in D♭ Major

Tones which sound the same but are notated differently are called enharmonics (D♭, C♯). The equivalent with words is "to, too, two." The key of D♭ major may also be written as C♯ major.

Practice Numbers 1 and 2 as preparation for reading the succeeding pieces in D♭ major. Practice hands separately at first. Also practice these patterns in D♭ minor.

1. Five-finger Position   ## 2. Primary Chords

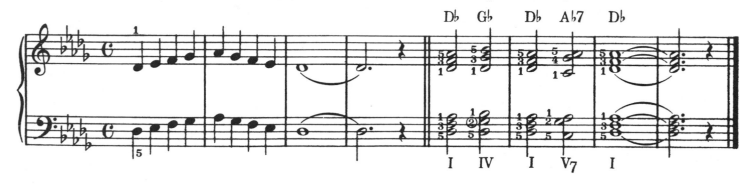

Practice Numbers 3, 4, and 5 as preparation for playing more difficult music. Practice hands separately at first.

Note: These scales and chords may also be practiced in minor keys. Refer to page 58.

3. D♭ Major Scale

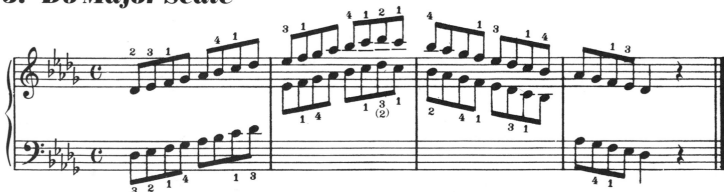

4. Triads and Inversions   ## 5. Dominant 7ths and Inversions

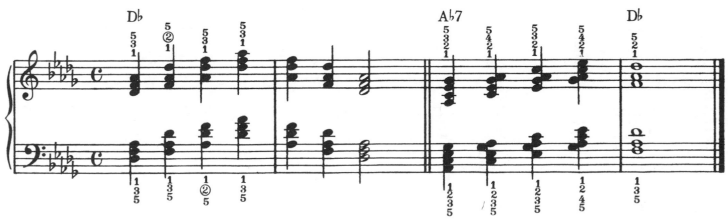

D♭ Reading Practice

f-p means to play **forte** the first time, then **piano** on the repeat.

Jacob's Ladder

See page 32 for various bass patterns. Improvise a different bass part for these verses:

2. Every round goes higher, higher . . .
3. Brother, do you love my Jesus . . .
4. If you love Him, you must serve Him . . .
5. We are climbing higher, higher . . .

Practice the following octave Preparatory Drills first with the right hand, then with the left hand, then with hands together. Transpose the drills to other keys.

Preparatory Drills

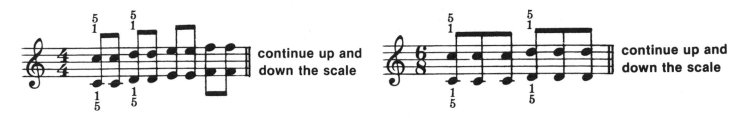

Vive la Compagnie

French Song

Folk Song

Also practice this piece using a waltz bass accompaniment. Refer to page 32.

Lullaby

Johannes Brahms (1833-1897)
arr. by J.W.B.

Also practice this piece using a broken chord bass accompaniment. Refer to page 32.

WP59

Reading in A♭ Major

Practice Numbers 1 and 2 as preparation for reading the succeeding pieces in A♭ major. Practice hands separately at first. Also practice these patterns in A♭ minor.

1. Five-finger Position

2. Primary Chords

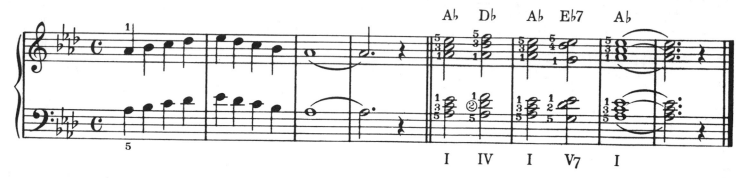

Practice Numbers 3, 4, and 5 as preparation for playing more difficult music. Practice hands separately at first.

Note: These scales and chords may also be practiced in minor keys. Refer to page 58.

3. A♭ Major Scale

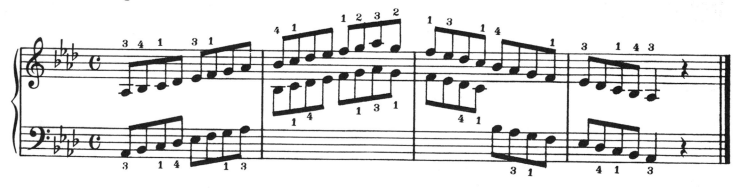

4. Triads and Inversions

5. Dominant 7ths and Inversions

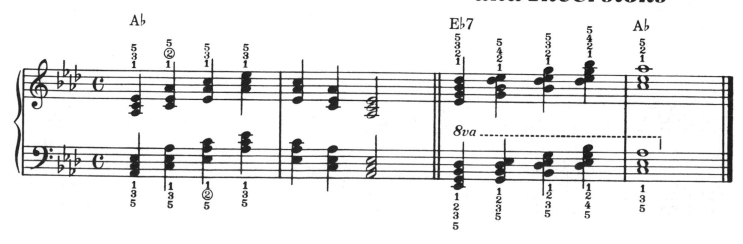

A♭ Reading Practice

Hymn Tune

Simeon B. Marsh
arr. by J.W.B.

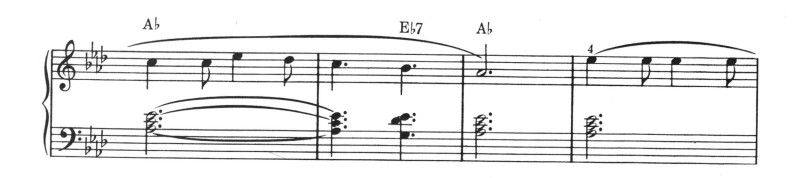

*Aura Lee**

Slowly, with feeling

Traditional

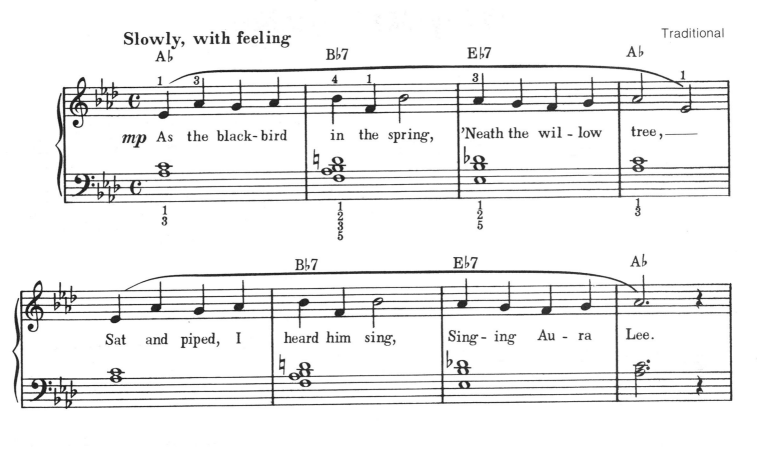

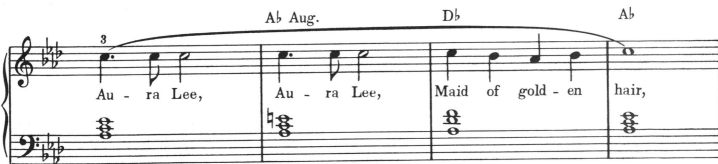

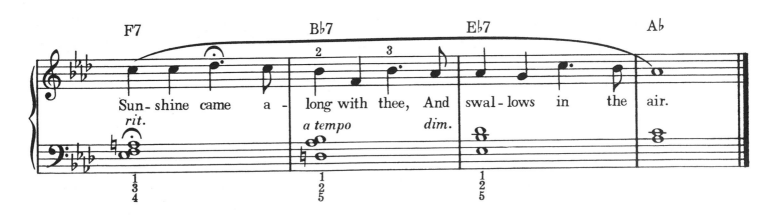

*Numerous versions of this popular serenade have been written over the years. It has been a favorite of college glee clubs and barbershops quartets. The West Point Cadets used the melody for **Army Blue,** and Elvis Presley's version, **Love Me Tender,** was an instant hit.

Tom Dooley

Folk Song

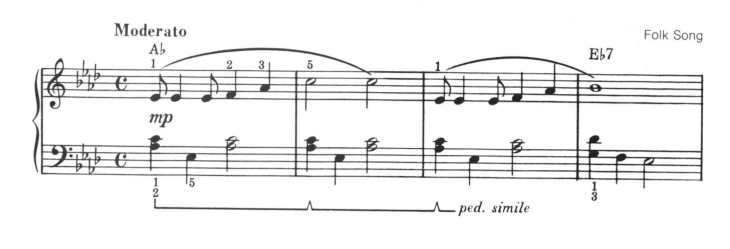

Merry Widow Waltz

from the opera ''The Merry Widow''

Franz Lehar (1870-1948)
arr. by J.W.B.

Reading in E♭ Major ...

Practice Numbers 1 and 2 as preparation for reading the succeeding pieces in E♭ major. Practice hands separately at first. Also practice these patterns in E♭ minor.

1. Five-finger Position

2. Primary Chords

Practice Numbers 3, 4, and 5 as preparation for playing more difficult music. Practice hands separately at first.

Note: These scales and chords may also be practiced in minor keys. Refer to page 58.

3. E♭ Major Scale

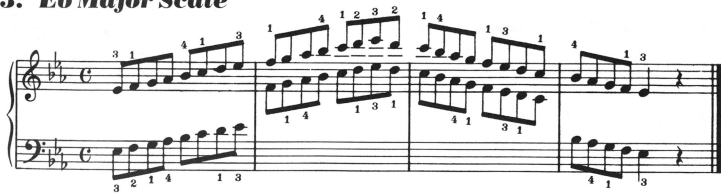

4. Triads and Inversions

5. Dominant 7ths and Inversions

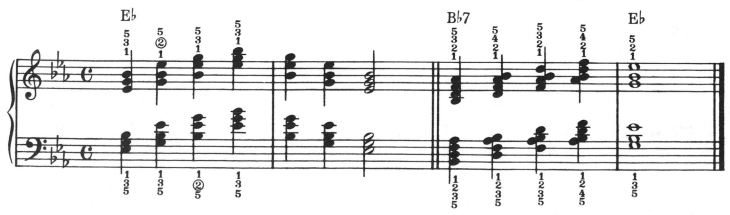

E♭ Reading Practice

Chiapanecas

Animato

Mexican Folk Song

Aria

from the opera "Marriage of Figaro"

Wolfgang A. Mozart (1756-1791)
arr. by J.W.B.

WP59

Dixieland Combo

Bright dixieland beat

arr. by J.W.B.

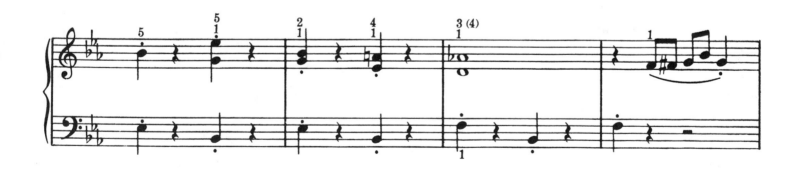

The Chromatic Scale

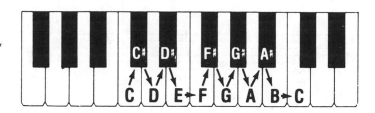

The chromatic scale is made of twelve half steps* (one octave). It may begin on any note.

Fingering Suggestions

1. Use your third finger on all the black keys.

2. Use your thumb on all the white keys except when two white keys are together. Then use your first and second fingers (1-2 or 2-1).

Practice the following chromatic scale Preparatory Drills. Play hands separately at first.

Preparatory Drills

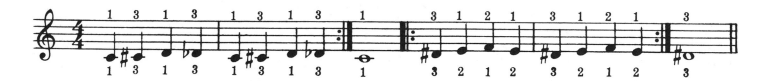

Chromatic Scale Study

For an explanation of half steps see page 188.

Night Riders

J.W.B.

Entry of the Gladiators

Julius Fucik (1872-1916)
arr. by J.W.B.

Tempo di marcia

Reading 16th Notes

A single sixteenth note receives one-fourth of a beat when a quarter note receives one beat.

A single sixteenth note has two flags. ♬

Two or more sixteenth notes are connected by a double beam. ♬

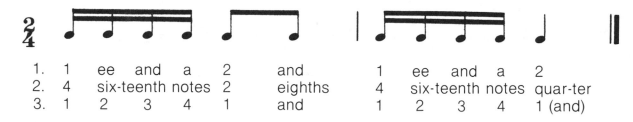

	2 4	3 4	4 4	Time Signatures	
♪	= ¼ beat		⅞	= ¼ beat rest	
♬	= ½ beat		⅞	= ½ beat rest	
♬♬	= 1 beat		⅊	= 1 beat rest	

Clap and count the following rhythms. Use any of the suggested ways for counting sixteenth notes.

1.	1	ee	and	a	2		and	1	ee	and	a	2
2.	4	six-teenth notes			2		eighths	4	six-teenth notes			quar-ter
3.	1	2	3	4	1		and	1	2	3	4	1 (and)

Count aloud while you play the following Etudes. Transpose to other keys.

16th Note Etudes

March of the Marionettes

J.W.B.

Clap and count the following rhythms *before* playing *Country Dance.*

1 and da 2 and 1 and da 2 and

Country Dance

Lively

Felix le Couppey (1811-1887)

Sonatina Form...

A sonatina usually has three movements (parts). The form of the first movement is often
A B A B Coda. Notice how the form is used in this sonatina.

In Italian, ''ina'' means little. The word sonat*ina* is used in the place of the word sonata, as a little
sonata. The word sonata was first used to mean music ''to be played'' (music for instruments).
Other music was ''to be sung'' (music for voices).

Sonatina

First movement from Op. 39, No. 1

Allegro

Frank Lynes (1853-1913)

Section A

Section B

legato

Coda

Dotted 8th Note Rhythm

A dot after a note increases the note's value by one-half. Dotted note rhythm patterns have a long-short ''feel.''

Four sixteenth notes equal one quarter note:

A *dotted eighth note* is equal to *three sixteenth notes*:

Clap and count the following rhythm. Use any of the suggested ways for counting the dotted eight note.

1. 1 - 2 - 3   4   1 - 2 - 3   4   half-note
2. long ___ short long ___ short   3 - 4
3. 1 and   a   2 and   a   3 - 4

Count aloud while you play the following Etude. Use any of the three ways given above for counting the dotted eight note rhythm. Play the Etude in other keys.

Dotted 8th Note Etude

Other common dotted note rhythm patterns are:

The form of this piece is **A B C A.**

Understanding musical form is an aid to learning and memorizing.

Country Gardens

Moderato

Section A

English Folk Dance

Section B

Section C

Section A

Frère Jacques

Folk Song
arr. by J.S.B.

Moderato

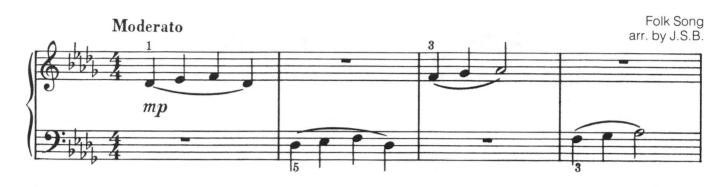

Blue Grass

J.W.B.

Augmented Triads

The word augment means to make larger.
An augmented triad is formed by raising the top note (5th) of a major triad a half step.

Practice the following Chord Drill as indicated. Play hands separately at first. Play the left hand an octave lower than written.

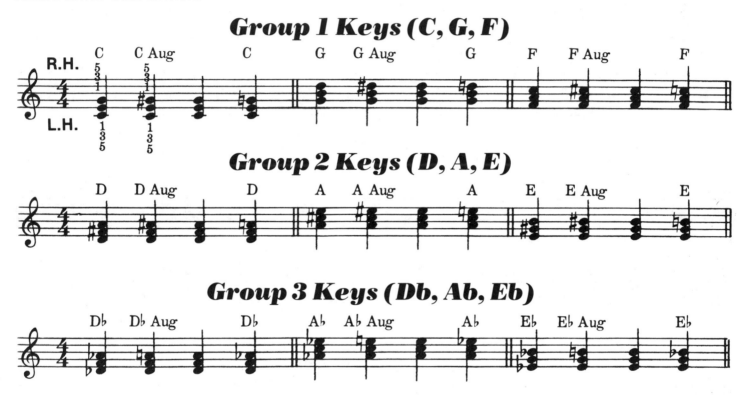

Group 1 Keys (C, G, F)

Group 2 Keys (D, A, E)

Group 3 Keys (Db, Ab, Eb)

Practice the following Chord Etude hands separately at first. Be sure to use the correct fingering. Write the name of each chord.

Major-Augmented Etude

Preparatory Drill

Practice the left hand Preparatory Drill
first with block chords.

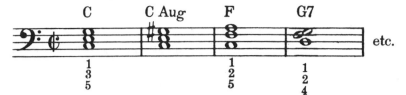

Lasting Love

Diminished Triads

The word diminish means to make smaller.
A diminished triad is formed by lowering the top note (5th) of a minor triad a half step.

Practice the following chord drill in the Group 1, 2, and 3 keys. Play hands separately at first. Play the left hand an octave lower than written.

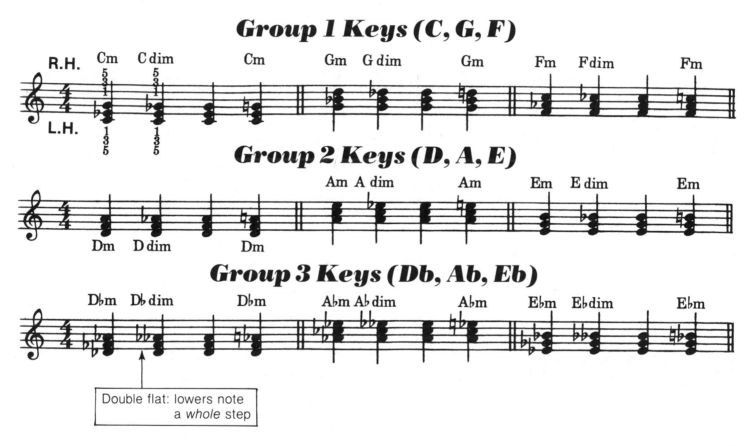

Practice the following Etude hands separately at first. Use the fingering that is given. Write the name of each chord.

Minor Diminished Etude

Lonesome

J.W.B.

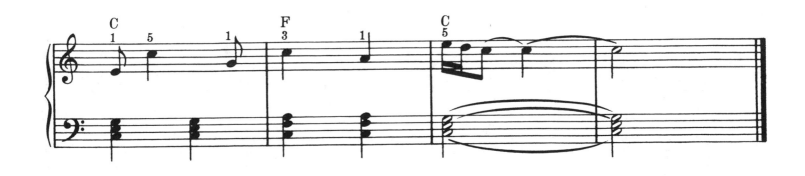

Reading in G♭ Major

The key signature of G♭ major may also be written enharmonically as F♯ major.

Practice Numbers 1 and 2 as preparation for reading the succeeding pieces in G♭ major. Practice hands separately at first. Also practice these patterns in G♭ minor.

1. Five-finger Position

2. Primary Chords

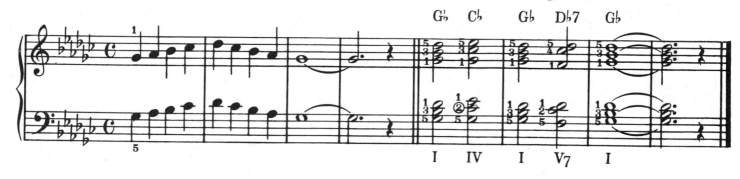

Practice Numbers 3, 4, and 5 as preparation for playing more difficult music. Practice hands separately at first.

Note: These scales and chords may also be practiced in minor keys. Refer to page 58.

3. G♭ Major Scale

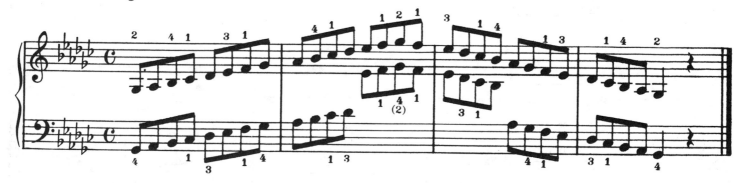

4. Triads and Inversions

5. Dominant 7ths and Inversions

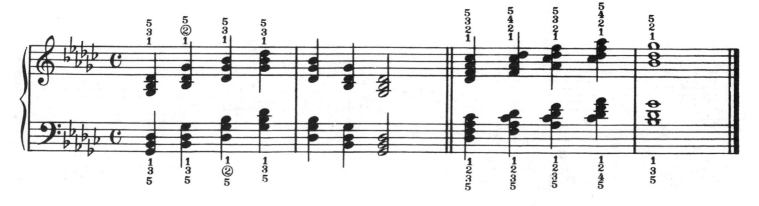

G♭ Reading Practice

The Streets of Laredo

Moderato

Traditional

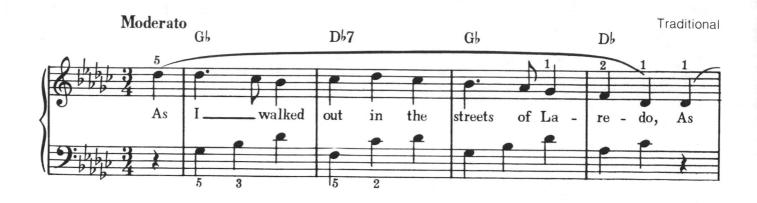

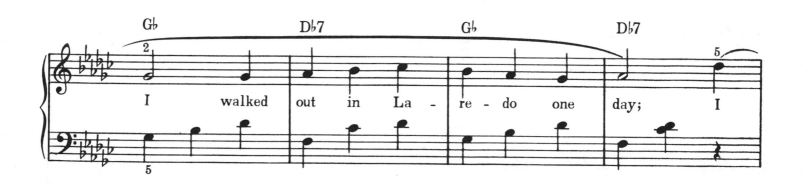

As I _____ walked out in the streets of La - re - do, As

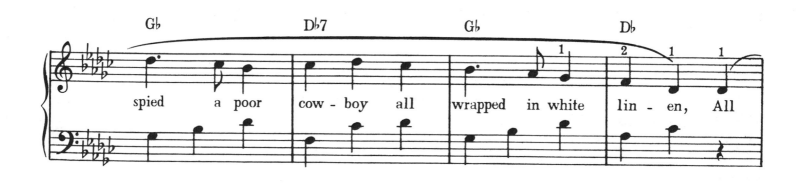

I walked out in La - re - do one day; I

spied a poor cow - boy all wrapped in white lin - en, All

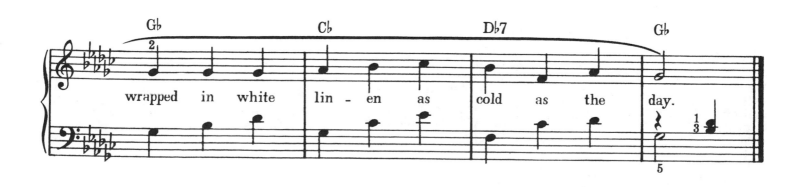

wrapped in white lin - en as cold as the day.

Ridin' at Daybreak

J.W.B.

Toccatina

J.S.B.

Minuet

Ignace J. Paderewski (1860-1941)
arr. by J.W.B.

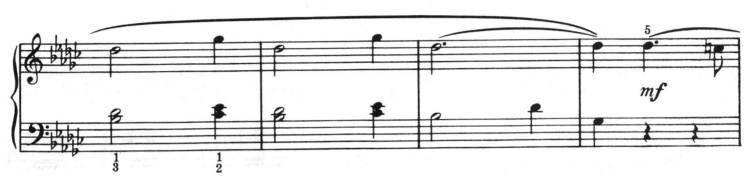

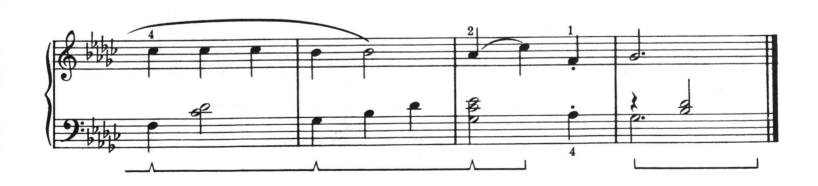

WP59

Reading in B♭ Major

Practice Numbers 1 and 2 as preparation for reading the succeeding pieces in B♭ major. Practice hands separately at first. Also practice these patterns in B♭ minor.

1. Five-finger Position

2. Primary Chords

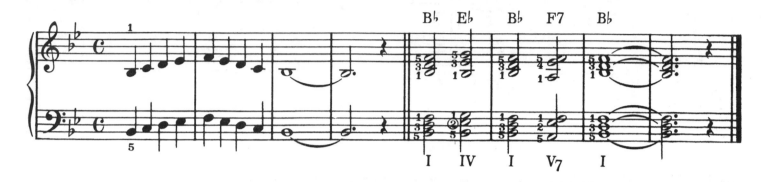

Practice Numbers 3, 4, and 5 as preparation for playing more difficult music. Practice hands separately at first.

Note: These scales and chords may also be practiced in minor keys. Refer to page 58.

3. B♭ Major Scale

4. Triads and Inversions

5. Dominant 7ths and Inversions

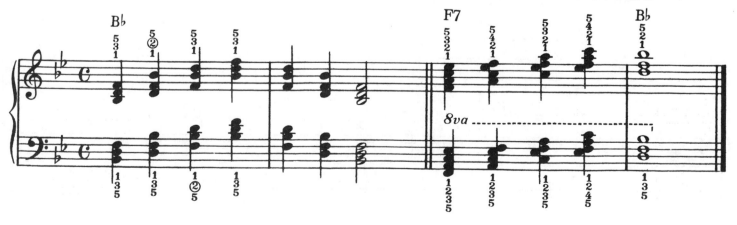

B♭ Reading Practice

Rock of Ages

Thomas Hastings (1784-1872)

Minuet

Johann Christian Bach (1735-1782)

All Through the Night

Old Welsh Air

Slowly

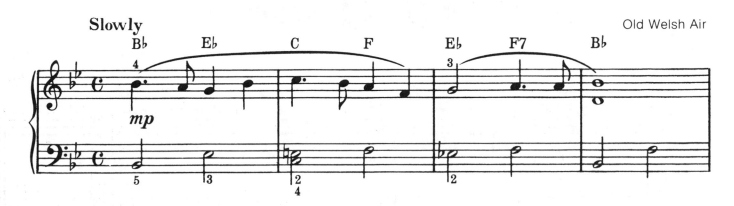

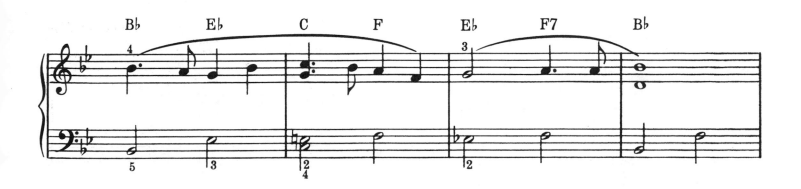

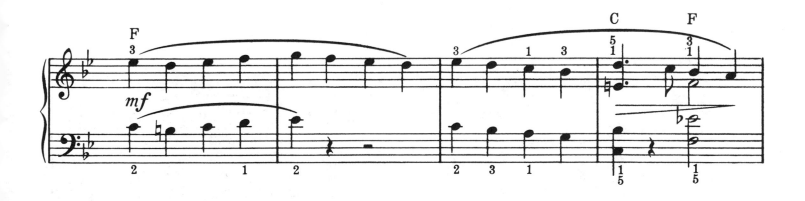

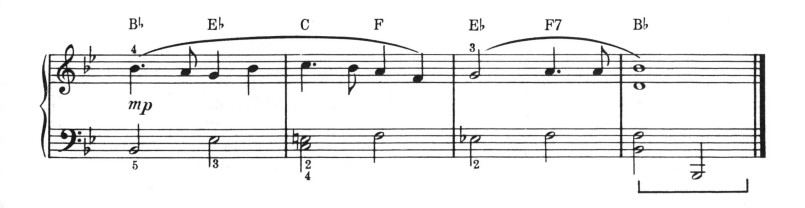

All Alone

Rock Ballad

J.W.B.

Reading in B Major

The key of B major may also be written enharmonically as C♭ major

Practice Numbers 1 and 2 as preparation for reading the succeeding pieces in B major. Practice hands separately at first. These patterns may also be played in B minor.

1. Five-finger Position   2. Primary Chords

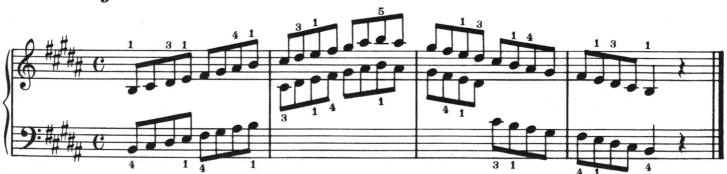

Practice Numbers 3, 4, and 5 as preparation for playing more difficult music. Practice hands separately at first.

Note: The scales and chords may also be practiced in minor keys. Refer to page 58.

3. B Major Scale

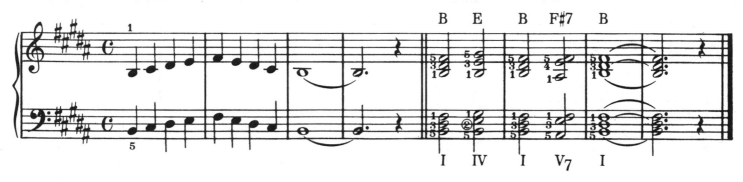

4. Triads and Inversions   5. Dominant 7ths and Inversions

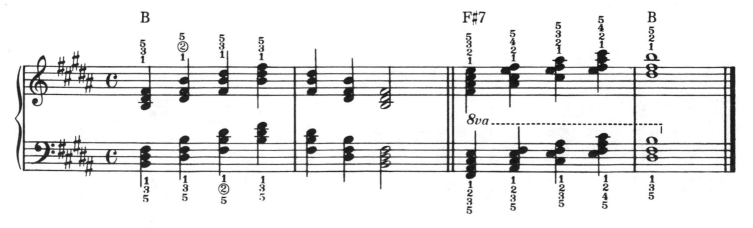

B Reading Practice

Hymn Tune

With spirit

George J. Webb (1803-1887)

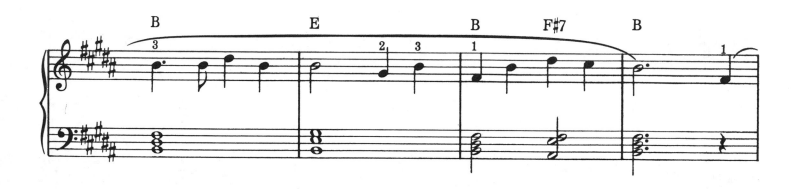

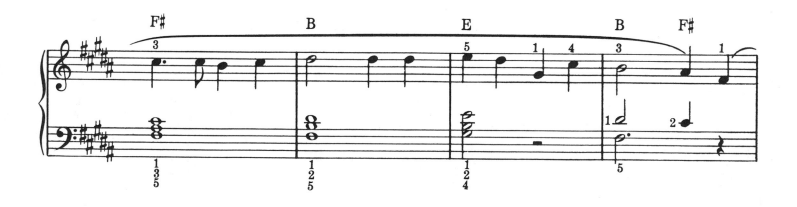

Practice the left hand alone to prepare for reaching up to the position in measures 3-4, 11-12, and 16. When played as written, the left hand crosses *over* the right hand.

Waltz

J.S.B.

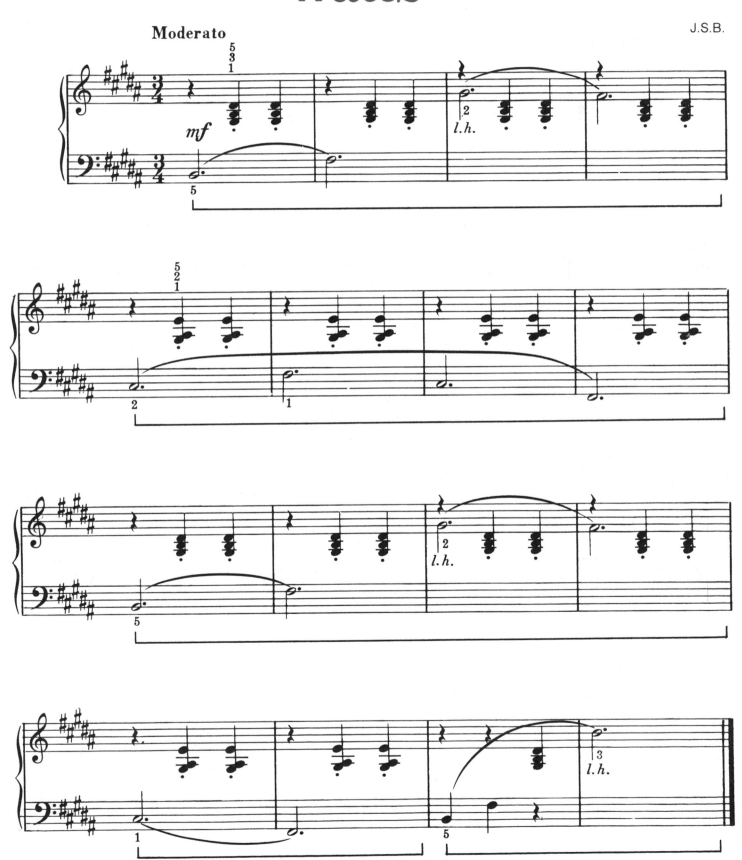

I've Been Working on the Railroad

Alla marcia

American Folk Song

I've been work-ing on the rail - road All the live-long day,

I've been work-ing on the rail - road To pass the time a - way;

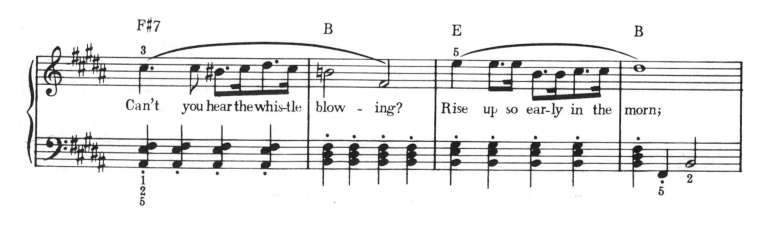

Can't you hear the whis-tle blow - ing? Rise up so ear-ly in the morn;

Section 3:
Shape Up!...

Basic Technic

This section contains exercises, scales, arpeggios, and etudes. Selections may be made according to need. They are designed to increase facility and promote evenness of touch and finger independence.

At first, play each new exercise on the following pages with a legato touch. Next, practice the exercises in the ways shown on these two pages. Repeat each exercise several times. Periodically review previously learned exercises. (The examples on these two pages use the opening notes of the Schmitt *Exercise* on page 138.)

Vary the touch...

a. staccato

b. legato-staccato

c. staccato-legato

d. legato-staccato

e. staccato-legato

f. accents

g. accents

h. legato-staccato combined

i. legato-staccato combined

Vary the Phrasing. . .

a. two-note slurs

b. four-note slurs

Vary the Rhythm. . .

a. dotted rhythm (long, short)

b. long, long, short

c. short, long, long

d. long, short

e. short, long

f. long, short

g. short, long

Vary the Tempo. . .

Practice in three tempos: slow, medium, fast.

Vary the Dynamics. . .

Use the whole range of dynamics from *pianissimo* to *fortissimo*. Also use gradual *crescendos* and *decrescendos*.

Vary the Key. . .

Transpose to other keys (major and minor).

Refer to the practice directions on page 136.

Preparatory Exercises

Op. 16

Aloys Schmitt (1788-1866)

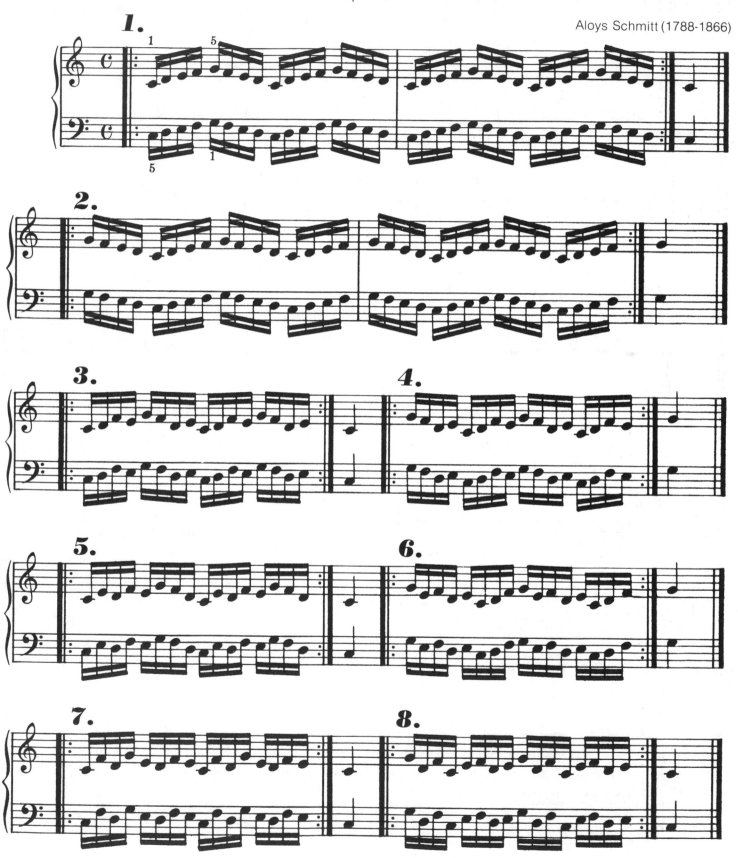

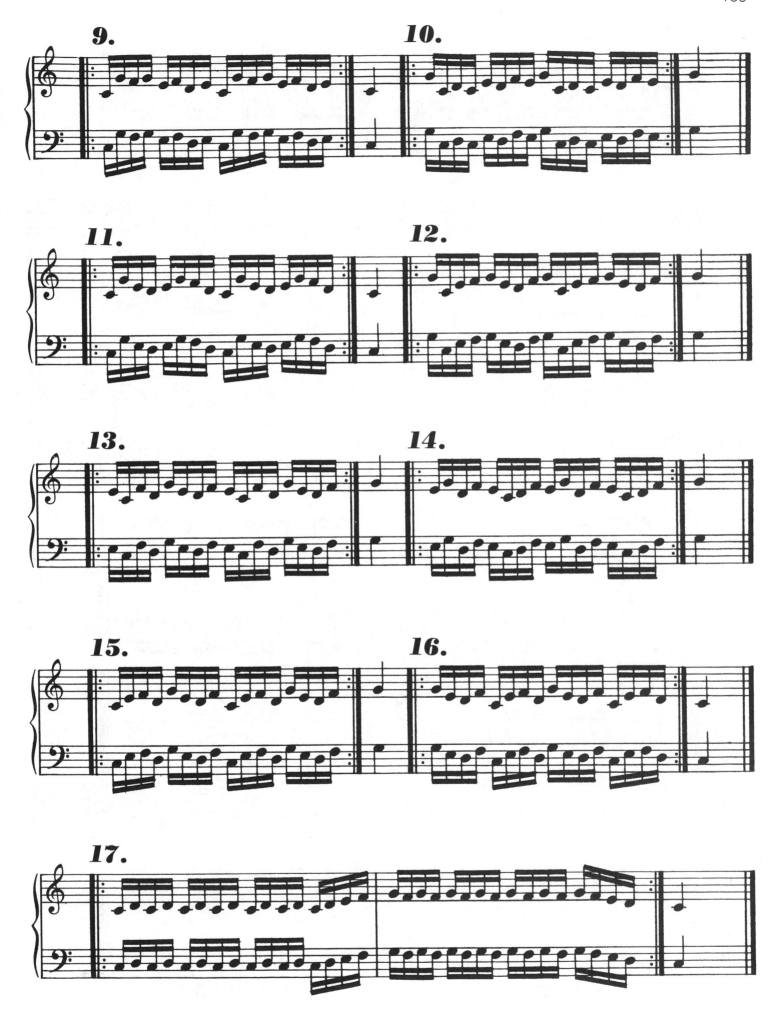

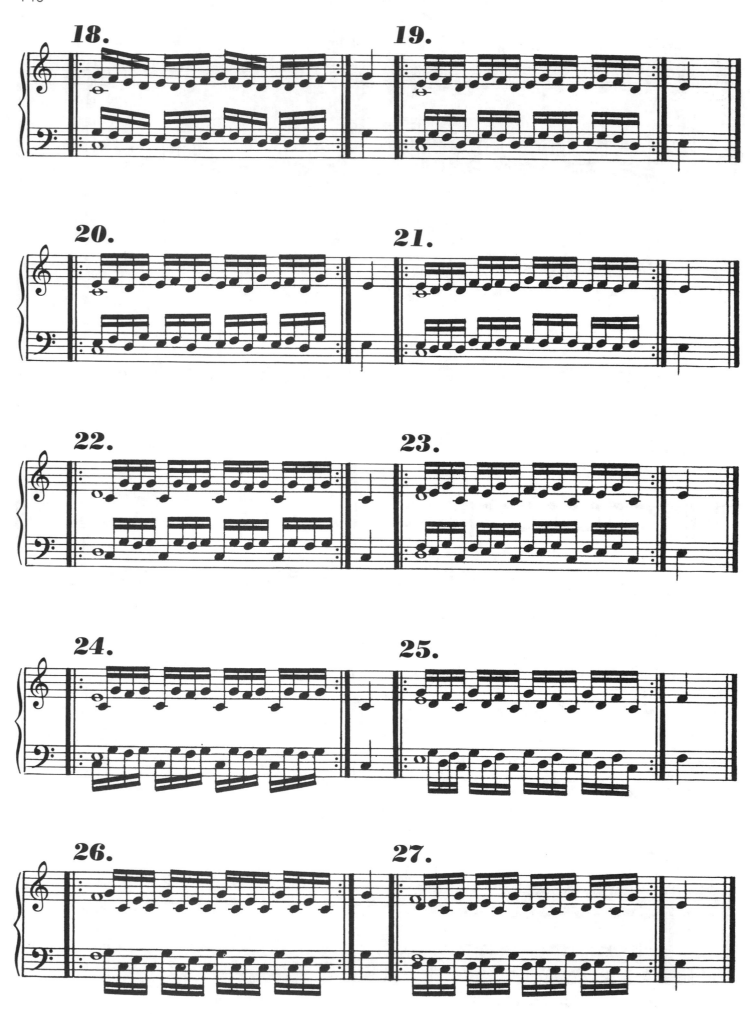

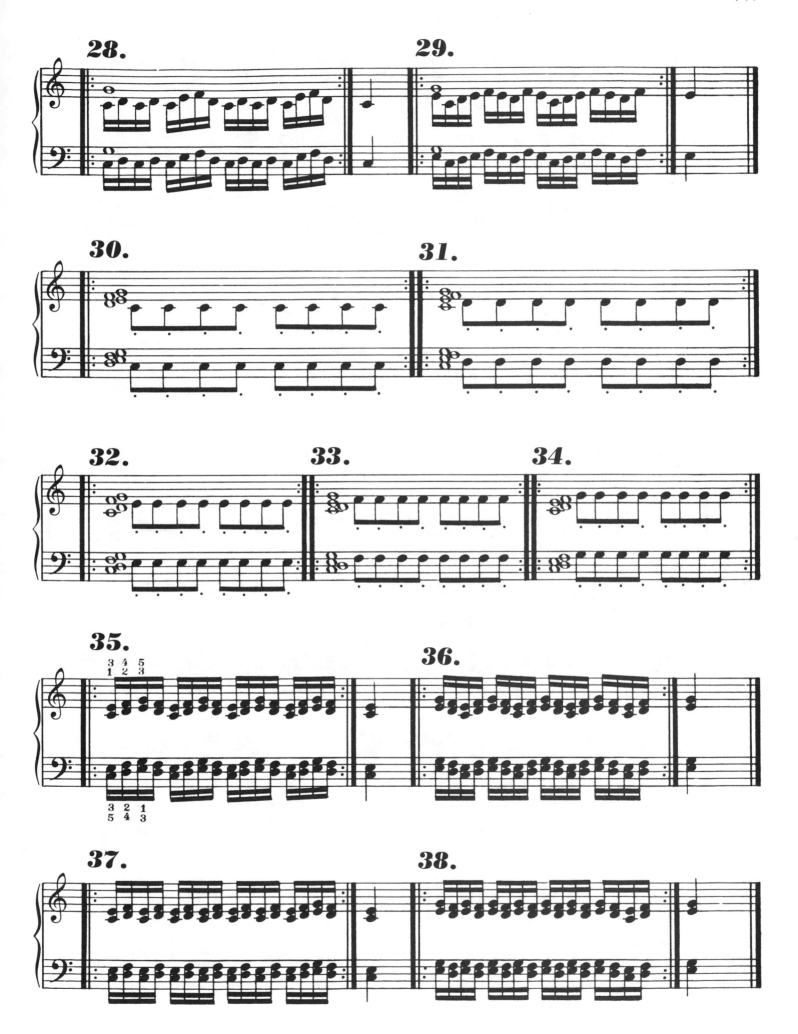

Refer to the practice directions on page 136.

Practical Finger Exercises

Op. 802

Carl Czerny(1791-1857)

Follow the practice directions given on pages 136-137. Play (repeat) each measure several times.

Introductory Exercises

Major Five-finger Positions

Josef Pischna (1826-1896)

Minor Five-finger Positions

The Virtuoso Pianist
Part 1

Follow the practice directions given on pages 136-137. Play both hands together, playing the left hand an octave lower than written. (The fingering above the notes is for the right hand; fingering below the notes is for the left hand.) Repeat each exercise several times. When each exercise is learned, proceed to the next one without stopping between exercises.

Charles Louis Hanon (1820-1900)

Scales
Major Scales and Major Triads

Harmonic Minor Scales and Minor Triads

Melodic Minor Scales

a minor

e minor

b minor

f# minor

c# minor

g# minor

d minor

g minor

c minor

f minor

b♭ minor

e♭ minor

Arpeggios

Major Arpeggios

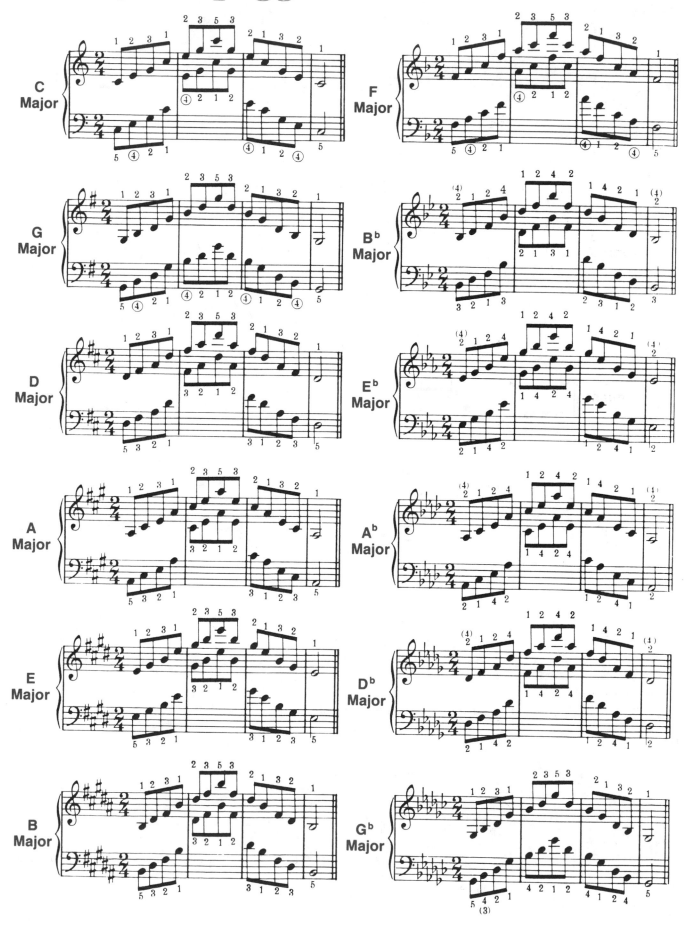

Minor Arpeggios

Studies

Carl Czerny (1791-1857)

5. Allegro

6. Allegretto

7. Allegro

8. Allegro moderato

Section 4: Attention Getters...

Piano Literature

The following selections are included to provide some pieces for further study. The number of pieces is purposely limited because it is difficult to select the appropriate grading for each student. You may wish to choose additional literature from the list on page 202.

Johann Sebastian Bach (1685-1750), a German composer, had numerous relatives who were musicians: from seven generations, 193 out of 200 were musicians. Bach's parents died when he was ten years old, and his oldest brother, Johann Christopher, raised him. His brother died when Johann Sebastian was fifteen. Following that, Johann Sebastian lived at the St. Michael School where he studied music and was a choirboy. At nineteen, Bach obtained a position as organist at a church in Arnstadt. Throughout his life he held positions at various churches and in royal courts, and for almost thirty years he was director of music at the St. Michael School in Leipzig. He was married twice and had twenty children, several of whom became well-known musicians. On his second wife's twenty-fifth birthday, he gave her (Anna Magdalena) a notebook containing pieces for members of his family to play. His best known easier clavier pieces come from this notebook. Bach was a prolific composer; his complete works fill forty-six large volumes containing choral music, concertos, orchestral and chamber works, and organ and clavier music.

Minuet in G Major (No. 1)

from "Notebook for Anna Magdalena"

J.S. Bach

Minuet in G Major (No. 2)

from "Notebook for Anna Magdalena"

J.S. Bach

Animato

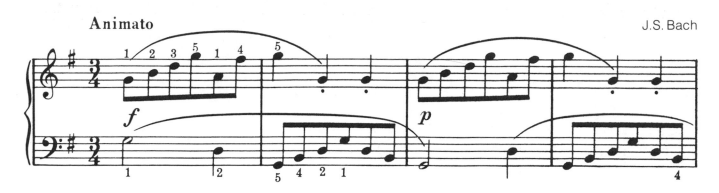

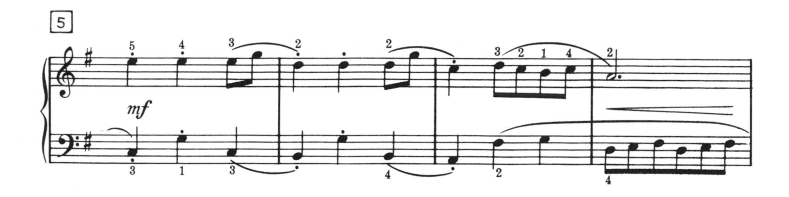

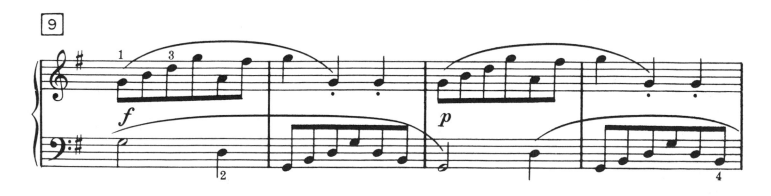

Franz Joseph Haydn

(1732-1809), an Austrian composer, studied singing, violin, and clavier in his youth, and became a choirboy at the Vienna Cathedral. He spent more than thirty years in the service of Prince Esterhazy, a Hungarian nobleman, at Eisenstadt. Haydn was a major influence in the development of the symphony, sonata, and string quartet. During his long life he composed approximately sixty-eight string quartets, more than fifty piano sonatas, two hundred songs, over one hundred symphonies, eighteen operas, a vast amount of church music, concertos, and many other works.

German Dance

Allegretto

Franz Joseph Haydn

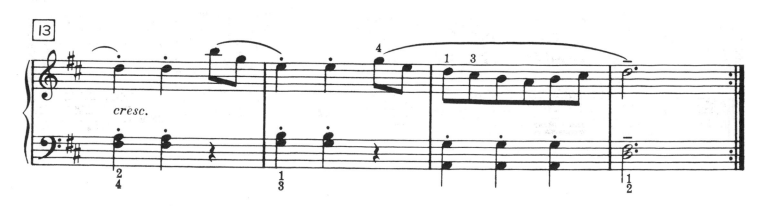

Scherzo

from "Sonata No. 3"

Franz Joseph Haydn

Wolfgang Amadeus Mozart (1756-1791), an Austrian composer and pianist, was a child prodigy. He was taught how to play the harpsichord and violin by his father, Leopold, and by the age of five he could play and compose music. When he was six his father arranged a debut for Wolfgang, and his sister, Nannerl. He then toured all over Europe displaying his remarkable musical ability in performing, sight reading, improvising, and composing. Mozart could write a complete symphony during a stagecoach ride, or write out a complicated score from memory after one hearing. During his brief life he wrote numerous symphonies, operas, concertos, songs, church music, chamber music, and keyboard music.

Minuet in C
K. 6

Wolfgang Amadeus Mozart

Allegro in B♭ Major

Wolfgang Amadeus Mozart

Ludwig van Beethoven

(1770-1827), a German composer, grew up in Bonn where he studied the violin and piano. Beethoven's father, a tenor employed as a chapel singer by the Archbishop-Elector of Bonn, was a stern taskmaster and drove young Ludwig to long hours of practice hoping that he would become a child prodigy like Mozart. Although Beethoven was obviously talented, he did not become a "marketable" child prodigy. In 1787 he visited Vienna where he played for Mozart who predicted an outstanding musical career for him. Beethoven hurried back to Bonn to attend his mother who had become ill. After his mother's death he remained at Bonn for five years as a viola player in the court opera orchestra. In 1792 he returned to Vienna and studied with Haydn for about a year. Around this time, Beethoven began to earn his living from the sale of compositions and from teaching. He became an honored and respected musician to many royal families (Prince Lichnowsky, Count Waldstein, Count Rasumovsky, etc.), and many works were dedicated to these noblemen. In his early thirties Beethoven experienced a hearing loss which later resulted in total deafness. The increasing deafness altered his character. He grew morose and suspicious and had frequent outbursts of temper. A prolific composer, Beethoven wrote thirty-two piano sonatas, five piano concertos, one violin concerto, an opera, a great quantity of chamber music, and many other works.

Russian Folk Song

Con spirito

Ludwig van Beethoven

German Dance

Ludwig van Beethoven

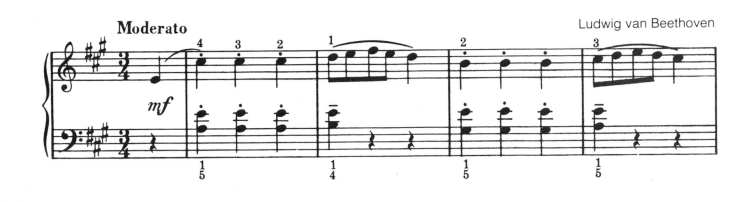

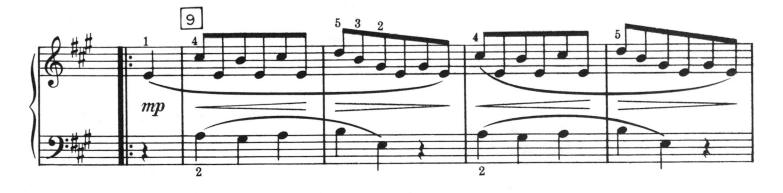

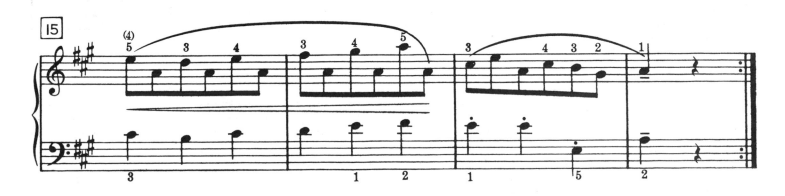

WP59

Für Elise*

Ludwig van Beethoven

*Although the original piece is written in $\frac{3}{8}$ meter, the resulting sound is the same.

Country Dance

Allegro moderato

Ludwig van Beethoven

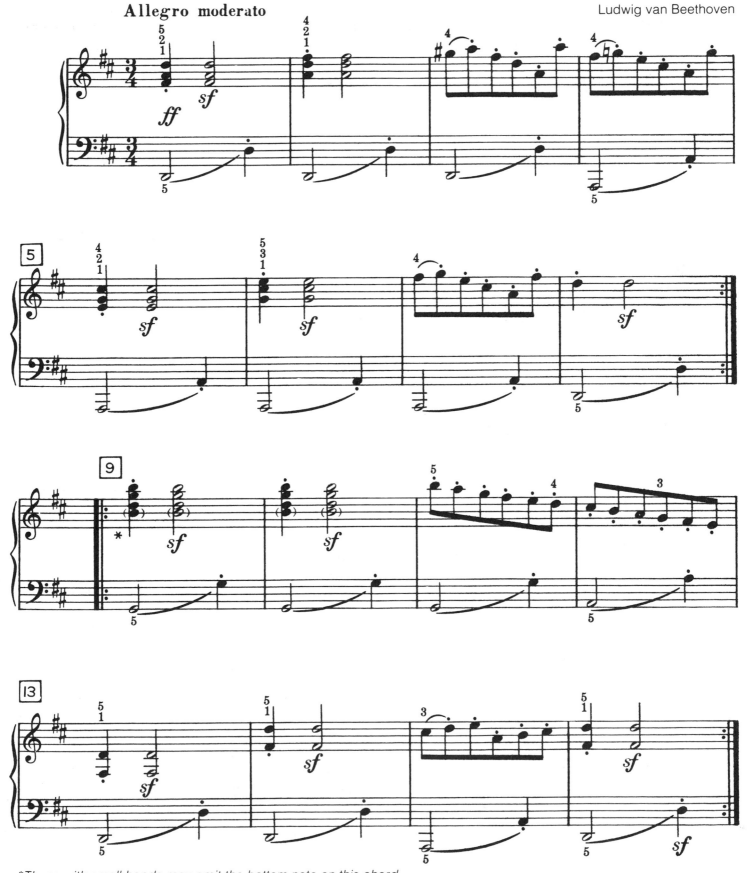

Those with small hands may omit the bottom note on this chord.

Robert Schumann (1810-1856), a German composer, was a child prodigy who played the piano when he was six years old and composed his first piano pieces when he was seven. His mother hoped he would become a lawyer, but he chose a music career and was allowed to study with the famous piano teacher, Friedrich Wieck, in Leipzig. Schumann injured his hand trying to gain a better technique by tying his fourth finger to a mechanical device to strengthen it. Because that made a career as a pianist impossible, he devoted his energies to composition. In 1840 he married Clara Wieck (his piano teacher's daughter) against her father's wishes. Clara was a brilliant pianist who performed many of Schumann's works. Schumann published a magazine called *The New Music Journal*. In it he was the first to report the importance of Chopin and Brahms. In 1850 Schumann was appointed Musical Director for the city of Dusseldorf. He held that position until 1853 when signs of insanity (which had been evident as early as 1833) compelled him to resign. From 1854 he spent the remainder of his life in an asylum at his own request. His compositions include symphonies, many piano works, a piano concerto, chamber music, songs, and choral works. The following piece is from the *Album for the Young* which Schumann wrote in 1848 as a birthday gift for his eldest daughter, Marie, who was then just seven years old.

The Merry Farmer

Op. 68, No. 10

Allegro animato

Robert Schumann

Felix Mendelssohn

(1809-1847), a German composer and pianist, was born in Hamburg of well-to-do parents. When Felix was three, his parents moved to Berlin where his schooling began with private tutors. He first performed in public at the age of nine; he began to compose at the age of twelve. Mendelssohn wrote his famous overture to *A Midsummer Night's Dream* when he was seventeen. He traveled extensively through England, Scotland, and the continent. His trips inspired him to write the descriptive overture *Fingal's Cave* and his *Symphony No. 3* ("Scotch") while in Scotland. A visit to Italy resulted in the *Symphony No. 4* ("Italian"). In 1829 Mendelssohn conducted Bach's *St. Matthew Passion* which was the first performance of a major work by Bach since his death almost eighty years earlier. The result was a revival of interest in Bach's music. Mendelssohn's interest in choral music inspired him to compose the oratorios *St. Paul* (1836), and for presentation in England, *Elijah* (1846). Mendelssohn was an extremely busy musician acting as a pianist, conductor of orchestras in Dusseldorf and Leipzig, and founder and dean of the Leipzig Conservatory, where he taught piano and composition. His health was never robust, and these taxing musical activities plus a whirlwind social life strained his constitution severely. He literally wore himself out and died of apoplexy at the age of thirty-eight. He was a prolific composer: his works include orchestral music, the *Violin Concerto in E Minor* (1844), piano concertos, choral and vocal music, chamber music, organ works, and well-known piano works such as the *Andante and Rondo Capriccioso, Variations Serieuses* and eight books of *Songs Without Words*.

Romanze

Felix Mendelssohn

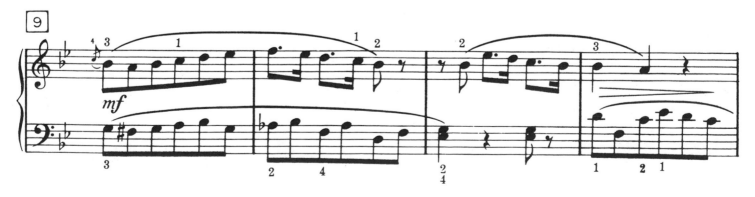

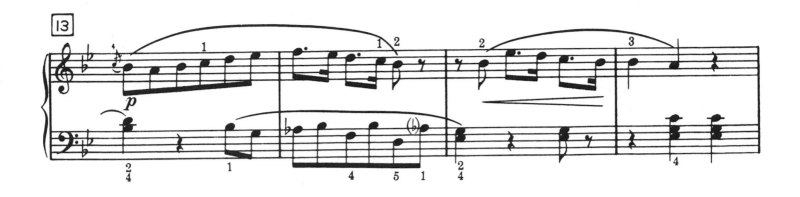

Cornelius Gurlitt (1820-1901), a German composer, was a pianist and organist. Although he wrote long works such as operas and sonatas for various instruments, he is mainly remembered for his piano miniatures written in the style of Schumann's *Album for the Young*.

Morning Song

Cornelius Gurlitt

Section 5:
Handy References...

Music Facts (Basic Theory)

Staffs, Clefs

The *staff* has five lines and four spaces.

To extend the staff, *ledger lines* are added above or below the staff to place additional notes.

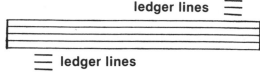

ledger lines

ledger lines

 The *treble clef* (or G clef) sign encircles the second staff line, identifying that as the first G above middle C.

𝄢 The *bass clef* (or F clef) sign indicates the F below middle C by the dots on either side of the fourth staff line.

Grand Staff

The *grand staff* is comprised of two sets of lines and spaces (two staves). The two staves are joined together by a *brace* and a *bar line*.

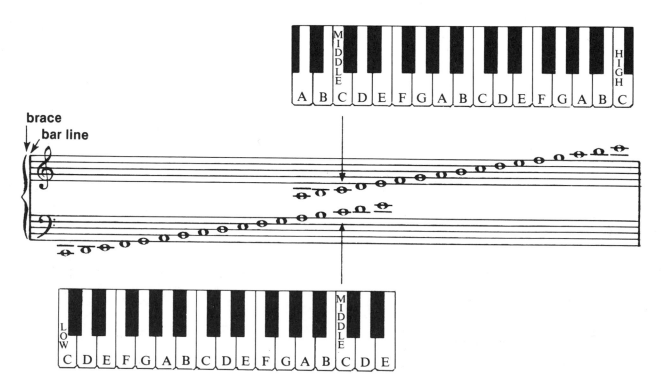

Measures, Bars

Music written on the staff is divided into *measures* (or bars) indicated by bar lines. A double bar is used at the end of a piece.

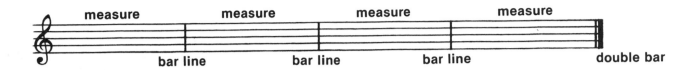

measure   measure   measure   measure

bar line   bar line   bar line   double bar

Accidentals

Accidentals are music signs placed in front of notes which temporarily alter their pitch. The most frequently used accidentals are the *sharp* (♯), *flat* (♭), and *natural* (♮) signs. These signs alter the pitch of notes *only* in the measure in which they are written.

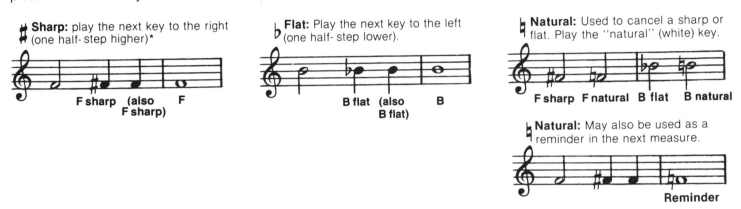

♯ **Sharp:** play the next key to the right (one half-step higher)*

F sharp   (also   F
           F sharp)

♭ **Flat:** Play the next key to the left (one half-step lower).

B flat   (also   B
          B flat)

♮ **Natural:** Used to cancel a sharp or flat. Play the "natural" (white) key.

F sharp   F natural   B flat   B natural

♮ **Natural:** May also be used as a reminder in the next measure.

Reminder

Time Signatures

The time signature is comprised of two numbers and is written at the beginning of a piece (or is written when the time changes from measure to measure). The *upper number* indicates the number of beats (or counts) per measure. The *lower number* indicates which kind of a note receives one *beat.*

2 2 beats in each measure
4 the quarter note (♩) gets one beat

3 3 beats in each measure
4 the quarter note (♩) gets one beat

4 4 beats in each measure
4 the quarter note (♩) gets one beat

6 beats in each measure
8 the eighth note (♪) gets one beat

A sign called common time (C) is often used in place of $\frac{4}{4}$: $C = \frac{4}{4}$

A sign called alla breve (₵), or "cut time" is often used in place of $\frac{2}{2}$: $₵ = \frac{2}{2}$

For an explanation of half steps see page 188.

Notes, Rests, Basic Rhythms $\left(\frac{2}{4}, \frac{3}{4}, \frac{4}{4}\right)$

Notes

o   whole note

𝅗𝅥   half note

♩   quarter note

♪   eighth note

𝅘𝅥𝅯   sixteenth note

Rests (indicate measured silence)

▬   whole rest

▬   half rest

𝄽   quarter rest

𝄾   eighth rest

𝄿   sixteenth rest

Basic rhythms in $\frac{2}{4}$, $\frac{3}{4}$, or $\frac{4}{4}$ time.

Count: 1   2   3   4

A dot after a note increases its value by one-half:

𝅗𝅥 = 2		𝅗𝅥. = 3
♩ = 1		♩. = 1½
♪ = ½		♪. = ¾

Basic dotted rhythms in $\frac{2}{4}$, $\frac{3}{4}$, or $\frac{4}{4}$ time.

Count: 1   2   3   4   Count: 1   and   2   and   Count: 1   and   da

Basic syncopated rhythms (stress on off-beat notes) in $\frac{2}{4}$, $\frac{3}{4}$, or $\frac{4}{4}$ time.

Count: 1   2   3   4   Count: 1   and   2   and   Count: 1   ee   and   da

Basic sixteenth-note rhythms in $\frac{2}{4}$, $\frac{3}{4}$, or $\frac{4}{4}$ time.

Count: 1 un and da   Count: 1   and   da   Count: 1 un and   Count: 1 and da

Notes, Rests, Basic Rhythms $\left(\frac{6}{8}\right)$

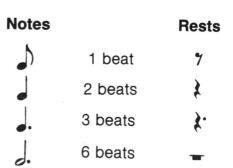

Notes

♪	1 beat
♩	2 beats
♩.	3 beats
𝅗𝅥.	6 beats

Rests

𝄾
𝄽
𝄽.
▬

Basic Rhythms in $\frac{6}{8}$ time.

Count: 1 2 3   4 5 6

Key Signatures

A key signature consists of the sharps or flats at the *beginning of each staff.* Rather than writing every sharp or flat as an accidental throughout a piece, the key signature is used for convenience. The key signature indicates two things:

1. The notes to be sharped or flatted throughout the entire piece.
2. The main key (tonality) of the piece.

Sharps and flats are always written in the same order on the staff.

The order of sharps is: **F C G D A E B**
The order of flats is: **B E A D G C F**
(*Note:* The sequence of flats is in reverse order of the sharps.)

The steps for identifying major sharp key signatures are:
1. Determine what the last sharp to the right is
2. Go *up* to the very next note (one half step). That is the name of the major key.

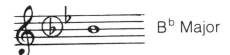
D Major

The steps for identifying major flat key signatures are:
1. Determine what the next-to-the-last flat is.
2. That is the name of the major key, with the exceptions of the key of C (no sharps or flats) and the key of F (one flat only).

B♭ Major

Every key signature applies to two keys, one in major and one in minor. A key signature with one sharp could represent G major or its relative E minor. The minor key is two alphabet letters lower (three half steps) than the major key name.

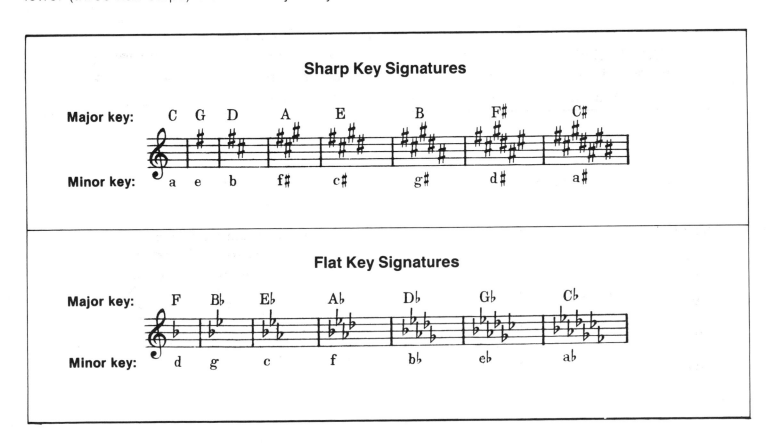

Half Step, Whole Step

The terms half step and whole step are used to *measure distances* on the piano keyboard.

Half Step	Whole Step
From one key to the nearest key with *no key in between* is a half step.	From one key to a neighbor key with *one key in between* is a whole step.

Major Scales

There are eight tones in a major scale called scale *degrees*. The scale degrees are arranged in a pattern of *whole steps* (1) and *half steps* (½). Roman numerals may be used to name scale degrees. Also, music terms may be used to name scale degrees: I, Tonic; II, Supertonic; III, Mediant; IV, Subdominant; V, Dominant; VI, Submediant; VII, Leading Tone.

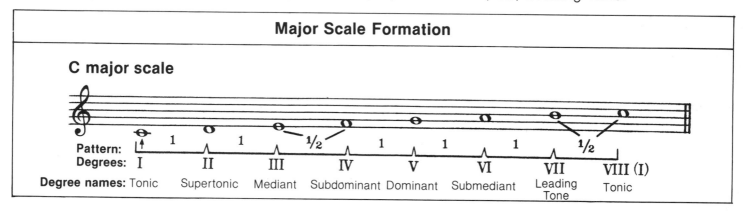

Major Scale Formation

C major scale

Pattern:	1	1	½	1	1	1	½
Degrees:	I	II	III	IV	V	VI	VII	VIII (I)
Degree names:	Tonic	Supertonic	Mediant	Subdominant	Dominant	Submediant	Leading Tone	Tonic

Scales and Modes

The word *mode* refers to the selection of tones arranged in a scale. These modes (major mode, minor mode, dorian mode, etc.) became established during the Middle Ages. They can be identified by reference to the white keys on the piano. The various scales may be identified by the number of pitches used and their intervallic relationships. A scale may have the same tones for both ascending and descending or it may have one series of tones ascending and another descending. Scales are constructed with half steps (½ step: the smallest interval in Western music), whole step (two ½ steps), or with larger intervals (1½ steps). In the scales below ‿ equals ½ step, ⋀ equals 1½ steps.

Major (Ionian mode)

Natural minor (Aeolian mode)　　　　　　　　　(Aeolian mode = white keys on the piano starting on A)

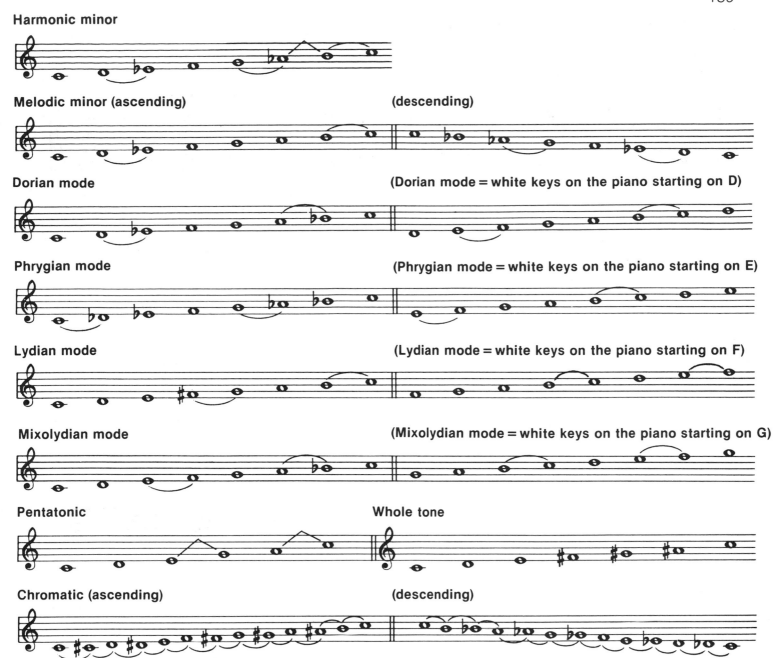

Intervals

An interval is the pitch relation or distance between two tones. The various types of intervals are major, minor, perfect, augmented, and diminished.

Major and Perfect Intervals

unison M second M third P fourth P fifth M sixth M seventh octave

Altered Intervals

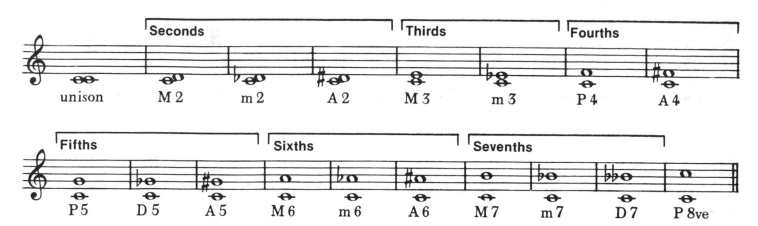

Chords

A chord is a combination of simultaneously-sounding tones. Chords provide *harmony* in music. Chords are "spelled" from the lowest tone upwards (C E G, not G E C) and are formed from musical alphabet skips (C E G, C E G B, etc.) The notes within chords form intervals. A triad (a three-note chord) has a root, third, and fifth; a seventh chord (a four-note chord) has a root, third, fifth, and seventh.

Chord symbols frequently are used to name the *type* of chord (major, minor, etc.). A chord symbol is the letter name of the chord (in root position) printed in music, usually above the melody: C, F, Dm, A Aug, etc. A single capital letter refers to a major chord (C = C major); a capital letter with a "m" after it refers to a minor chord (Cm = C minor); a capital letter with "Aug" after it refers to an augmented chord (C Aug = C augmented); a capital letter with "dim" after it refers to a diminished chord (C dim = C diminished).

These four different triads are used most frequently: *major* triad, *minor* triad, *augmented* triad, and *diminished* triad.

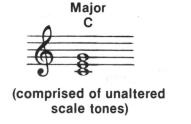

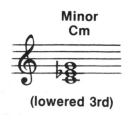

A chord can be consructed on each note of the scale. Triads I, IV, and V in major scales are called *primary triads* and are major. Triads ii, iii, and vi are minor. Triad vii° is diminished.

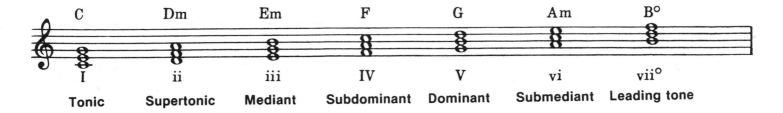

Inversions of Chords

Any chord may be *inverted* (rearranged). A triad is inverted by moving the root note to the top or middle.

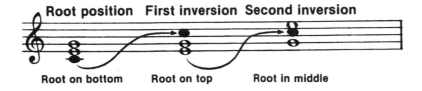

Dominant 7th Chord

The dominant seventh chord is built on the *fifth* tone of the scale. The dominant seventh chord has a root, third, fifth, and seventh.

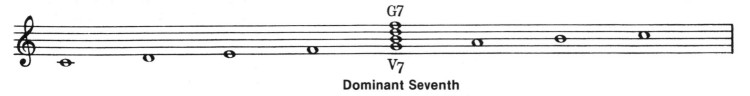

The dominant seventh chord has four positions because it is a four-note chord: root position, first inversion, second inversion, third inversion.

Each inversion of the dominant seventh chord has an interval of a *second*. The *root* of the inverted chord is the *top* note of the interval that is a second. Understanding this will aid in identifying inverted seventh chords.

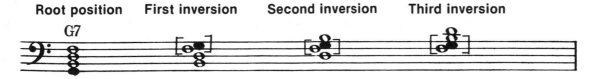

Playing Primary Chords on the Piano

For harmonization, primary chords are frequently played on the piano in this manner: I, root position; IV, second inversion, V⁷, first inversion (with the fifth omitted).

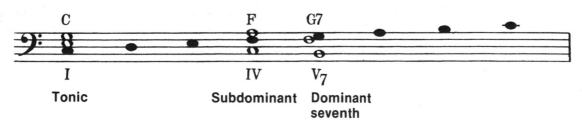

Four-Part Harmony

Four-part harmony is the basis for most music of the eighteenth and nineteenth centuries. This means a vertical construction of four chord tones (one being doubled), and a horizontal movement of four different melodic voices (soprano, alto, tenor, bass). Essentially the spacing of tones within chords is either in *close* or *open* structure. When the three upper voices (or parts) are as close together as possible (soprano and tenor not exceeding an octave apart), the spacing is called close position. Any spacing that exceeds a distance greater than an octave between soprano and tenor is called open position.

Close position   **Open position**

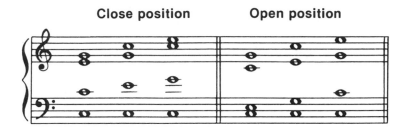

Doublings

It is obvious that one of the three tones in a triad must be doubled to write four-part harmony. The extra tone is usually obtained by doubling the root in root position chords (as in the examples above). For other rules applying to doublings of first and second inversion chords consult a formal theory text.

Cadences

Music is quite analogous to literature because of its essentially linear, horizontal (left to right) motion. The horizontal, melodic movement of music is punctuated by phrases, whereas the vertical (chordal) structure culminates in *cadences* (various points of rest). Below are examples of frequently used cadences.

(a) The *authenic cadence* is comparable to a full stop or a period in punctuation, and consists of a V-I harmonic progression.

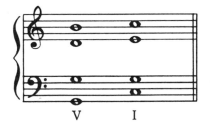

V   I

(b) The *half cadence* acts like a comma, indicating a partial stop in an unfinished statement. It ends on a V chord, however approached.

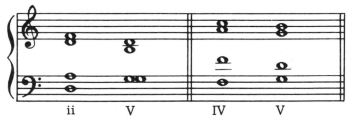

ii   V   IV   V

(c) The *plagal cadence* is the next most frequently used progression for a full stop or final repose after the authentic cadence. It is also the "amen" sound used in hymns and consists of a IV-I progression.

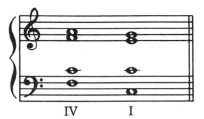

IV   I

(d) The *deceptive cadence* is a frequent substitute for the authentic cadence. As an alternative to V-I, V-vi (deceptive cadence) is often used.

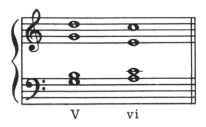

V   vi

Nonharmonic Tones (Non-chord tones)

The texture of music is comprised of melodic tones and rhythms which are interwoven. Some of these tones appear as factors of chords and some do not. *Nonharmonic tones* are tones that become foreign to the prevailing harmony during the course of melodic movement. Below are examples of frequently used nonharmonic tones.

(a) A *passing tone* is a dissonant tone (non-chordal tone) interpolated generally between two consonant tones. It usually occurs on a rhythmically weak beat and is approached and left by step without change of direction. The passing tone (or tones) may be either diatonic or chromatic.

(b) An *auxiliary tone* (also called neighboring tone or embellishment) is a dissonant tone of weak rhythmic value which serves to ornament a stationary tone (either from above or below). It is approached and left by step with change of direction.

(c) An *anticipation,* as its name implies, is an advance sounding of the subsequent tone. It acts as an up-beat to the tone anticipated. It is a dissonant, rhythmically weak tone, usually approached by step, and becomes consonant without moving as the harmony resolves to it.

(d) An *escape tone* (or éschappée) is a dissonant, rhythmically weak tone, approached by step and left by leap.

(e) An *appoggiatura* (from the Italian verb *appoggiare,* to lean) is a dissonant tone on a rhythmically strong beat which is usually approached by leap and left by step.

(f) A *suspension* (or retardation) is the prolongation of a chordal tone of which it is a member, into a chord of which it is not a member. The three elements of the suspension are frequently referred to as the *preparation (consonant tone), suspension* (dissonant tone on a rhythmically strong beat), and *resolution* (usually by step downward).

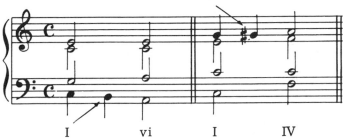

Circle of Keys

This diagram is called the circle of keys. The sharps are arranged from the top, moving clockwise. The flats are arranged from the top, moving counter-clockwise.

There are 15 major keys: 7 sharp keys, 7 flat keys, and 1 key with no sharps or flats.

There are 15 relative minor keys.

The keys with two names at the bottom of the circle are called enharmonic.

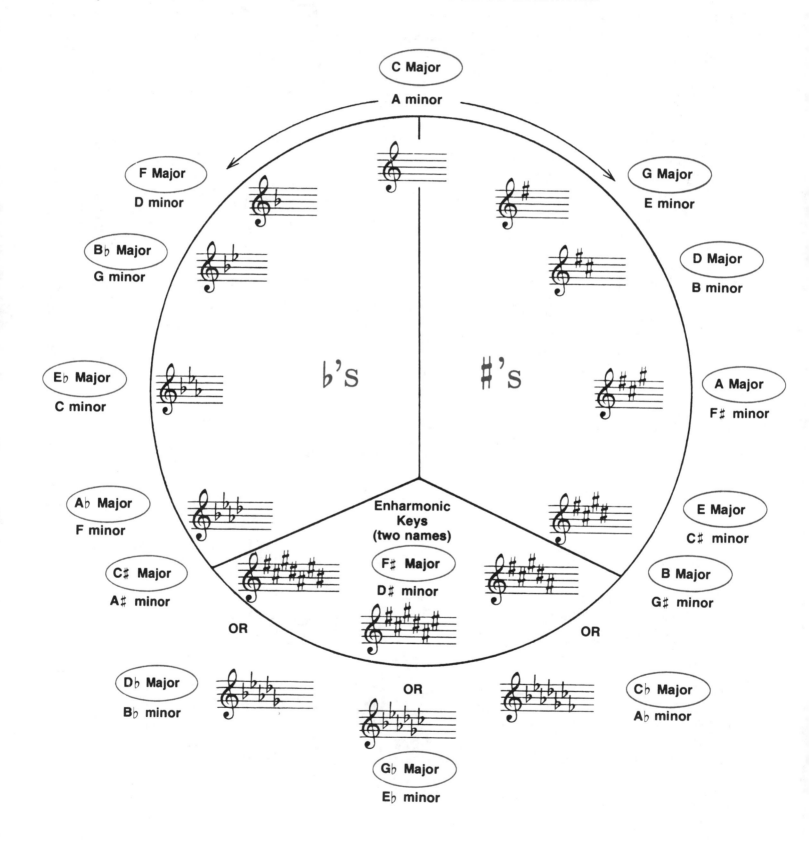

Chord Dictionary

It is difficult to label this chord. Occasionally, the term half-diminished seventh is used. It is a minor seventh chord with a lowered fifth (may be shown as Cm7-5 or Cm7♭5).

General Reference Books on Music

Piano

Barthold, Kenneth van, and David Buckton. *The Story of the Piano.* Edinburgh: T. & A. Constable Ltd., 1975.

Cooke, Charles. *Playing the Piano for Pleasure.* New York: Simon and Schuster, 1960. Paper.

Friskin, James, and Irwin Freundlich. *Music for the Piano.* New York: Dover Publications, Inc., 1973. Paper.

Gerig, Reginald R. *Famous Pianists and Their Technique.* Washington: Robert B. Luce, 1974.

Gillespie, John. *Five Centuries of Keyboard Music.* New York: Dover Publications, Inc., 1972. Paper.

Grover, David S. *The Piano: Its Story, from Zither to Grand.* London: Robert Hale, 1976.

Hinson, Maurice. *Guide to the Pianist's Repertoire.* Bloomington, Indiana: Indiana University Press, 1977.

Hinson, Maurice. *Guide to the Pianist's Repertoire—Supplement.* Bloomington, Indiana, 1980.

Hollis, Helen Rice. *The Piano: A Pictorial Account of Its Ancestry and Development.* London: David and Charles, Ltd., 1975.

Kirby, Frank E. *A Short History of Keyboard Music.* New York: The Free Press, 1966.

Mach, Elyse. *Great Pianists Speak for Themselves.* New York: Dodd, Mead and Co., 1980.

Marcus, Adele. *Great Pianists Speak with Adele Marcus.* Neptune, New Jersey: Paganiniana Publications, Inc., 1979.

Schoenberg, Harold C. *Great Pianists from Mozart to the Present.* New York: Simon & Schuster, Inc., 1963.

Dictionaries and Encyclopedias

Apel, Willi, and Ralph Daniel. *The Harvard Brief Dictionary of Music.* Cambridge, Mass.: Harvard University Press, 1960. Paper.

Barlow, Harold, and Sam Morgenstern. *A Dictionary of Musical Themes.* New York: Crown Publishers, 1948.

Grove, Sir George, ed. *Grove's Dictionary of Music and Musicians,* 6th Edition, edited by Eric Blom. New York: St. Martin's Press, 1981.

Hindley, Geoffrey, ed. *The Larousse Encyclopedia of Music.* New York: The World Publishing Co., 1971.

Osborne, Charles. *The Dictionary of Composers.* New York: Taplinger Publishing Co., 1978.

Randel, Don Michael, ed. *Harvard Concise Dictionary of Music.* Cambridge, Mass.: Harvard University Press, 1978. Paper.

Slonimsky, Nicolas, ed. *Baker's Biographical Dictionary of Musicians,* 6th Edition. New York: G. Schirmer, Inc., 1978.

Westrup, J.A., and F.L. Harrison. *The New College Encyclopedia of Music,* Revised Edition. New York: W.W. Norton & Co., Inc., 1976.

Introductory Books on Music

Christ, DeLone, Winold. *Involvement with Music.* New York: Harper & Row, 1975.

Gillespie, John. *The Musical Experience,* 2nd Edition. Belmont, Calif.: Wadsworth Publishing Company, Inc., 1973.

Hickock, Robert. *Music Appreciation,* 2nd Edition. Reading, Mass.: 1975.

Machlis, Joseph. *The Enjoyment of Music,* 3rd Edition. New York: W.W. Norton & Co., Inc., 1970.

Thompson, William. *Music for Listeners.* New York: Prentice-Hall, Inc., 1978.

Histories

Grout, Donald J. *A History of Western Music,* Revised Edition. New York: W.W. Norton & Co., Inc., 1973.

Hansen, Peter S. *An Introduction to Twentieth Century Music,* 3rd Edition. Boston: Allyn and Bacon, Inc., 1971.

Lang, Paul Henry, and Otto Bettmann. *A Pictorial History of Music.* New York: W.W. Norton & Co., Inc., 1960.

Longyear, Rey M. *Nineteenth-Century Romanticism in Music.* Englewood Cliffs, N.J.: Prentice-Hall, Inc., 1969. Paper.

Palisca, Claude V. *Baroque Music.* Englewood Cliffs, N.J.: Prentice-Hall, Inc., 1968. Paper.

Pauly, Reinhard G. *Music in the Classic Period,* 2nd Edition. Englewood Cliffs, N.J.: Prentice-Hall, Inc., 1973. Paper.

Pincherle, Marc. *An Illustrated History of Music.* London: Macmillan Company, Ltd., 1962.

Young, Percy M. *A Concise History of Music.* New York: David White, Inc., 1974.

Theory

Form

Fontaine, Paul. *Basic Formal Structures in Music.* New York: Appleton-Century-Crofts, 1967.

Kohs, Ellis B. *Musical Form.* Boston: Houghton Mifflin Co., 1976.

Harmony

Benjamin, Horvit, Nelson. *Techniques and Materials of Tonal Music,* 2nd Edition. Boston: Houghton Mifflin Co., 1979.

Christ, DeLone, Kliewer, Rowell, Thomson. *Materials and Structure of Music I.* Englewood Cliffs, N.J.: Prentice-Hall, Inc., 1967.

Christ, DeLone, Kliewer, Rowell, Thomson. *Materials and Structure of Music II.* Englewood Cliffs, N.J.: Prentice-Hall, Inc., 1967.

Ottman, Robert. *Elementary Harmony,* 2nd Edition. Englewood Cliffs, N.J.: Prentice-Hall, Inc., 1970.

Piston, Walter. *Harmony,* 4th Edition. Revised and expanded by Mark DeVoto. New York: W.W. Norton & Co., Inc., 1978.

Introductory Books

Harder, Paul. *Basic Materials in Music Theory.* Boston: Allyn and Bacon., Inc., 1970.

Howard, Bertrand. *Fundamentals of Music Theory.* New York: Harcourt, Brace & World, Inc., 1978.

Wharram, Barbara. *Elementary Rudiments of Music.* Oakville, Ontario, Canada: The Frederick Harris Music Co., Ltd., 1969.

Special Interest Books

American Music

Hitchcock, H. Wiley. *Music in the United States: A Historical Introduction.* Englewood Cliffs, N.J.: Prentice-Hall, Inc., 1969. Paper.

Chamber Music

Hinson, Maurice. *The Piano in Chamber Ensemble.* Bloomington, Indiana: Indiana University Press, 1978.

Ulrich, Homer, *Chamber Music,* 2nd Edition. New York: Columbia University Press, 1966.

Concerto

Young, Percy M. *Concerto.* Boston: Crescendo Publishers, 1968.

Harpsichord and Clavichord

Russell, Raymond. *The Harpsichord and Clavichord.* London: Faber and Faber, 1959.

Instruments

Kendall, Allan. *The World of Musical Instruments.* London: The Hamlyn Publishing Group, Ltd., 1972.

Musical Ability

Shuter, Rosamund. *The Psychology of Musical Ability.* London: Methuen, 1968.

Opera

Davidson, Gladys. *The Barns Book of the Opera.* New York: Barnes & Noble., Inc., 1962.

Grout, Donald J. *A Short History of Opera,* 2nd Edition. New York: Columbia University Press, 1965.

The Simon and Shuster Book of Opera. New York: Simon and Shuster, 1977.

Piano Pedagogy

Bastien, James. *How to Teach Piano Successfully,* 2nd Edition. San Diego, California: General Words and Music, Distributed by Kjos West, 1977. Paper.

Enoch, Yvonne, and James Lyke. *Creative Piano Teaching.* Champaign, Illinois: Stipes Publishing Co., 1977.

Chronological List of Keyboard Composers

Baroque Period (1600-1750)

Jean Baptiste Lully, French (1632-1687)
Henry Purcell, English (1658-1695)
François Couperin, French (1668-1733)
Georg Philipp Telemann, German (1681-1767)
Jean-Philippe Rameau, French (1683-1764)
Johann Sebastian Bach, German (1685-1750)
Domenico Scarlatti, Italian (1685-1757)
George Frideric Handel, German (1685-1759)

Classical Period (1775-1825)

Wilhelm Friedemann Bach, German (1710-1781)
Carl Philipp Emanuel Bach, German (1714-1788)
Johann Christian Bach, German (1735-1782)
Johann Philipp Kirnberger, German (1721-1783)
Joseph Haydn, Austrian (1732-1809)
Muzio Clementi, Italian (1752-1832)
Wolfgang Amadeus Mozart, Austrian (1756-1791)
Daniel Gottlieb Türk, German (1756-1813)
Ludwig van Beethoven, German (1770-1827)
Antonio Diabelli, Italian (1781-1858)
Friedrich Kuhlau, German (1786-1832)

Romantic Period (1800-1900)

Franz Schubert, German (1797-1828)
Felix Mendelssohn, German (1809-1847)
Friedrich Burgmüller, German (1806-1874)
Frédéric Chopin, Polish (1810-1849)
Robert Schumann, German (1810-1856)
Franz Liszt, Hungarian (1811-1886)
Stephen Heller, German (1813-1888)
Fritz Spindler, German (1817-1905)
Theodor Kullak, German (1818-1882)
Louis Kohler, German (1820-1886)
Cornelius Gurlitt, German (1820-1901)
César Franck, French (1822-1890)
Johannes Brahms, German (1833-1897)
Camille Saint-Saëns, French (1835-1921)
Modest Mussorgsky, Russian (1839-1893)
Peter Tchaikowsky, Russian (1840-1893)
Edvard Grieg, Norwegian (1844-1908)
Vladimir Rebikoff, Russian (1866-1920)

Contemporary Period (1900-   )

Edward MacDowell, American (1861-1908)
Claude Debussy, French (1862-1918)
Alexander Gretchaninoff, Russian (1864-1956)
Erik Satie, French (1866-1925)
Alexander Scriabin, Russian (1872-1915)
Max Reger, German (1873-1916)
Sergei Rachmaninoff, Russian (1873-1943)
Arnold Schoenberg, Austrian (1874-1951)
Maurice Ravel, French (1875-1937)
Manuel de Falla, Spanish (1876-1946)
Ernst von Dohnányi, Hungarian (1877-1960)
Ernest Bloch, Swiss (1880-1959)
Béla Bartók, Hungarian (1881-1945)
Joaquin Turina, Spanish (1882-1949)
Igor Stravinsky, Russian (1882-1971)
Anton Webern, Austrian (1883-1945)
Alfredo Casella, Italian (1883-1947)
Alban Berg, Austrian (1885-1935)
Heitor Villa-Lobos, Brazilian (1887-1959)
Jacques Ibert, French (1890-1962)
Sergei Prokofieff, Russian (1891-1953)
Darius Milhaud, French (1892-1974)
Paul Hindemith, German (1895-1963)
George Gershwin, American (1898-1937)
Francis Poulenc, French (1899-1963)
Alexander Tcherepnin, Russian (1899-1977)
Aaron Copland, American (1900-   )
Ernst Křenek, Austrian (1900-   )
Aram Khachaturian, Russian (1903-1978)
Dmitri Kabalevsky, Russian (1904-   )
Dmitri Shostakovich, Russian (1906-1975)
Paul Creston, American (1906-   )
Ross Lee Finney, American (1906-   )
Elliot Carter, American (1908-   )
Samuel Barber, American (1910-1981)
Gian Carlo Menotti, American (1911-   )
Norman Dello Joio, American (1913-   )
Vincent Persichetti, American (1915-   )
David Diamond, American (1915-   )
Alberto Ginastera, Argentine (1916-   )
Leonard Bernstein, American (1918-   )
Ned Rorem, American (1923-   )
Robert Starer, American (1924-   )
Carlisle Floyd, American (1926-   )
Robert Muczynski, American (1929-   )
Stanley Babin, Israeli (1932-   )

Musical Terms and Symbols

TEMPO   Indicates rate of speed

Largo—broadly, very slowly
Lento—slowly
Adagio—slowly, leisurely
Andante—a walking pace, flowing
Andantino—slightly faster than andante
Moderato—moderately
Allegretto—quickly, but not as fast as allegro
Allegro—at a quick pace, lively
Vivace or Vivo—lively
Presto—very fast
Prestissimo—faster than presto

Changing Tempos

Accelerando (accel.)—to become faster
A tempo—resume original tempo
Mosso—motion
Moto—motion, con moto—with motion, quicker
Rallentando (rall.)—gradually slowing in speed
Ritardando (rit.)—becoming slower
Ritenuto (riten.)—immediate slowing

DYNAMICS   Pertaining to the volume of sound

Pianissimo (pp)—very soft
Piano (p)—soft
Mezzo piano (mp)—moderately soft
Mezzo forte (mf)—moderately loud
Forte (f)—loud
Fortissimo (ff)—very loud
Sforzando (sfz)—strong accent

Changing Dynamics

Crescendo (cresc.)—growing louder
Decrescendo (decresc.)—growing softer
Diminuendo (dim., dimin.)—growing softer

STYLE   The character or mood of the composition

Animato—animated, with spirit
Brio—vigor, spirit
Cantabile—singing
Dolce—sweetly
Espressivo (espress.)—with expression, feeling
Giocoso—humorously
Grazioso—gracefully
Legato (leg.)—smoothly, connected tones
Leggiero—lightly
Maestoso—majestically
Marcia—as a march
Portamento—slightly disconnected tones
Scherzando—playfully
Sostenuto—sustained
Staccato (stacc.)—disconnected tones
Tenuto (ten.)—held, sustained
Tranquillo—calm, quiet, tranquil

MISCELLANEOUS TERMS

Coda—ending
Con—with
D.C. (Da Capo)—go to the beginning
D.C. al Fine—repeat from the beginning to the end
(Fine)
D.S. (Dal Segno)—the sign 𝄋
D.S. al Fine—repeat from the sign to the end (Fine)
Fermata—pause, or hold the note 𝄐
Fine—the end

Loco—in normal location or pitch register
Meno—less
Molto—much
Non—not
Piu—more
Poco—a little
Poco a poco—little by little, gradually
Sempre—always
Simile—in a similar way
Subito (sub.)—suddenly, at once
Troppo—too much

NOTES & RESTS

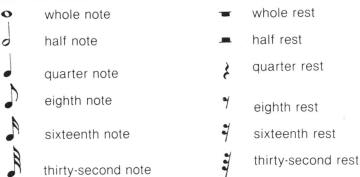

𝅝 whole note		whole rest	
𝅗𝅥 half note		half rest	
𝅘𝅥 quarter note		quarter rest	
𝅘𝅥𝅮 eighth note		eighth rest	
𝅘𝅥𝅯 sixteenth note		sixteenth rest	
𝅘𝅥𝅰 thirty-second note		thirty-second rest	

grace note, to be played quickly

arpeggiated, or rolled chord

SIGNS

♯   sharp
♭   flat
♮   natural
𝄐   fermata
staccato
slur, or tie; depends on situation
𝄪   double sharp
♭♭   double flat
8va   octave
portamento
triplet
first and second endings
stress, accent, strong accent
𝄴   (common time)—4 beats to the measure
𝄵   (alla breve)—2 strong beats to the measure
repeat sign
tied notes

slurred notes

Ped *, P., ⎣__⎦   ⋀_⋀   pedal indications

Glossary

A 440 (acoustics)
A above middle C, equal to 440 vibrations per second. An accepted standard pitch.

Absolute music
Music composed for its own sake, devoid of extra-musical implications.

Absolute pitch
The ability to correctly identify sounds (pitches) heard.

Acoustics
The science of sound.

Anacrusis
Synonomous with up-beat, indicating a melody beginning before the first complete measure.

Antiphonal
Opposing bodies of sound, such as one choir answered by another.

Arrangement
The adaptation of a composition for an instrument or instruments other than those specified in the original form.

Atonality
The absence of tonal (key) feeling.

Augmentation
The lengthening of note values.

Bitonality
The use of two different keys simultaneously.

Cacophony
Harsh or discordant sounds.

Cadenza
An extended solo passage to display the performer's technical skill; usually appears in a concerto before the conclusion of the first movement.

Chamber music
Music for a small group of soloists, intended for intimate performance in a small room rather than a large auditorium.

Chord
A simultaneous sounding of three or more tones.

Chromatic
Tones foreign to a key. A scale comprised of semitones.

Concerto
A composition for one or more solo instruments with orchestra.

Consonance
A state of relative rest between tones that produces an agreeable effect.

Contrapuntal
In the style of counterpoint. Two or more individual melodic parts combined at the same time.

Counterpoint
"Note against note." The art of writing independent melodies against each other.

Development
The evolution or elaboration of a melody or motive.

Development section
The middle portion in a sonata-allegro movement where the themes and motives are elaborated on.

Diatonic
The natural succession of tones within a scale, excluding chromatic alterations.

Diminution
The shortening of note values.

Dissonance
A combination of tones that produces unrest and generally creates a disagreeable effect.

Dodecaphonic music
Music composed in a twelve-tone series; used synonomously with *twelve-tone music* and *serial music.*

Embellishment
Melodic ornamentation consisting of trills, grace notes, runs, etc.

Enharmonic
The same pitch given to two different letter names.

Ensemble
Any combination or group of singers and/or instrumentalists.

Episode
A digression from the main thematic material (in fugal form). A transitory passage (in sonata-allegro form).

Equal temperament (acoustics)
A system of tuning whereby the octave is divided into twelve equal semitones.

Euphony
Harmonic, pleasant sounding.

Exposition
The initial section of a musical form in which the basic thematic material is presented. The first portion of a sonata-allegro movement (exposition, development, recapitulation).

Form
The structure of a musical composition.

Figured bass
A system of musical shorthand whereby chords are indicated by figures placed below the bass line.

Fugue
A highly sophisticated form of imitative counterpoint comprised of a subject (theme) presented in one voice part and answered (imitated) by another voice or voices in close succession.

Glissando
Gliding or sliding. In keyboard music, playing a series of keys by dragging a finger (or fingers) along the keyboard.

Harmony
Consonant sounds that produce a pleasing whole. The science of chord and chordal progressions.

Homophony, homophonic
A musical style in which the melody predominates and the accompaniment is subordinate.

Linear motion
Scale-wise (step-wise) motion. Horizontal motion.

Metronome
A device to indicate the exact tempo of a composition. Invented by John Maelzel in 1815, the metronome indicates any desired number of beats per second.

Motive
A brief fragment of a musical theme or subject which may have special melodic and/or rhythmic character.

Movement
A main section of a large work such as a first movement of a sonata, concerto or symphony.

Musicology
The scholarly study of music, particularly in the field of history, as differentiated from the art of composition, performance, etc.

Notation
The graphic representation of music by symbols that indicate pitch and duration of time.

Percussive effect
Strident, sharp, biting sound.

Phrase
A natural division of the melodic line, punctuated by some form of cadence (melodic, harmonic, or rhythmic close).

Polyphony, polyphonic
Simultaneous sounding of two or more melodies.

Polytonal, polytonality
The use of several different keys simultaneously.

Recapitulation
The reprise or restatement of material already presented. The third portion of the first movement in sonata-allegro form (exposition, development, recapitulation).

Retrograde
Moving backwards, i.e. beginning with the last note and ending with the first.

Rubato
A free style of playing in which one note may be extended at the expense of another for expressive purposes.

Serial music
See *Dodecaphonic music*.

Sequence
The repetition of a melodic pattern at successively higher or lower intervals.

Sonority
Richness or fullness of sound.

Tonality
The gravitation of a musical composition around a key or tonal center.

Touch
The manner in which the keys of the piano are depressed to produce different tone qualities.

Transcription
See *Arrangement*.

Triad
A chord of three pitches consisting of the root, third, and fifth of a scale.

Tune
A melody or air. The art of adjusting the pitch of an instrument.

Twelve-tone technique
See *Dodecaphonic music*.

Virtuosity
Brilliant display of technical facility.

Piano Music Collections

The following books provide a variety of music from which selections may be made according to interest and need. The "Easy" categories are suggestions for students in the beginning stages; the "Intermediate" categories are for students with several years of study. Any of the following books may be used as supplements to *Piano: 2nd Time Around*.

Piano Literature Collections...

Easy

Agay, Denes (ed.)	*Easy Classics to Moderns*	Consolidated
Anthony, George (ed.)	*Composers for the Keyboard, Easy Vol. 1*	Presser
Bastien, James (ed.)	*First Piano Repertoire Album*	Kjos West
Bastien, James (ed.)	*Easy Piano Classics*	Kjos West
(collection)	*Album of Easy Pieces by Modern Composers for the Piano*	Kalmus/Belwin

Intermediate

Agay, Denes (ed.)	*The Joy of Baroque*	Yorktown
Agay, Denes (ed.)	*The Joy of Romantic Piano*	Yorktown
Agay, Denes (ed.)	*Piano Recital, Intermediate to Early Advanced*	Amsco
Anthony, George (ed.)	*Composers for the Keyboard, Intermediate Vol. 1*	Presser
Banowetz, Joseph (ed.)	*The Pianist's Book of Baroque Treasures*	GWM/Kjos
Banowetz, Joseph (ed.)	*The Pianist's Book of Classic Treasures*	GWM/Kjos
Banowetz, Joseph (ed.)	*The Pianist's Book of Early Romantic Treasures*	GWM/Kjos
Banowetz, Joseph (ed.)	*The Pianist's Book of Late Romantic Treasures*	GWM/Kjos
Banowetz, Joseph (ed.)	*The Pianist's Book of Early Contemporary Treasures*	GWM/Kjos
Bastien, James (ed.)	*Piano Literature, Vol. 3*	GWM/Kjos
Bastien, James (ed.)	*Piano Literature, Vol. 4*	GWM/Kjos
Bergenfeld, Nathan (ed.)	*Renaissance to Rock*	Amsco
Brisman, Heskel (ed.)	*Baroque Dynamite*	Alfred
Brisman, Heskel (ed.)	*Classical Classics*	Alfred
(collection)	*Easy Keyboard Music from Two Centuries, Vol. 1*	Henle
(collection)	*Easy Piano Solos by Classical & Romantic Composers, Vol. 1*	Henle
Palmer & Lethco (eds.)	*Creating Music at the Piano, Book 6*	Alfred

Sonatina Collections...

Easy

Bastien, Jane S.	*First Sonatinas*	GWM/Kjos
Bastien, Jane S.	*Sonatinas for the Seasons*	GWM/Kjos

Intermediate

Agay, Denes (ed.)	*The Joy of Sonatinas*	Yorktown
Bastien, James (ed.)	*Sonatina Favorites, Books 1-3*	Kjos West
Frey, Martin (ed.)	*The New Sonatina Book, Book 1*	Schott
Kohler & Klee (eds.)	*Sonatina Album*	Schirmer
Kohler & Ruthardt (eds.)	*Sonatina Album, Vols. 1 & 2*	Peters
Small, Allan (ed.)	*Sonatina Album*	Alfred

Classic Theme Arrangements

Easy

Bastien, James (arr.)	*Classic Themes by the Masters*	Kjos West
Small, Allan (arr.)	*42 Famous Classics*	Alfred

Intermediate

Agay, Denes (arr.)	*Treasury of Popular Classics*	Amsco
Grant, Lawrence	*World's Favorite Popular Classics for Piano*	Ashley
Small, Allan (arr.)	*Romantic Cream*	Alfred

Supplementary Collections...

Easy
Bastien, Jane S. (arr.) .... *Favorite Melodies the World Over, Level 1* .... Kjos West

Intermediate
Agay, Denes (arr.) .... *Highlights of Familiar Music for Piano, Vols. 1 & 2* .... Presser
Agay, Denes (arr.) .... *The Joy of Piano* .... Yorktown
Bastien, Jane S. (arr.) .... *Favorite Melodies the World Over, Level 2* .... Kjos West

Pop Albums . . .

Easy
Bastien, James and Jane S. ..... *Pop Piano Styles, Level 2* .... Kjos West
Bastien, James .... *Country, Western 'n Blues, Book 1* .... GWM/Kjos
Bastien, Jane S. .... *Pop, Rock 'n Blues Books 1 & 2* .... GWM/Kjos
Stecher/Horowitz/Gordon ..... *Rock With Jazz, Books 1 & 2* .... Schirmer
Stecher/Horowitz/Gordon ..... *Rock, Rhythm & Rag, Books 1 & 2* .... Schirmer

Intermediate
Agay, Denes .... *The Joy of Jazz* .... Yorktown
Agay, Denes .... *The Joy of Boogie and Blues* .... Yorktown
Bastien, James and Jane S. ..... *Pop Piano Styles, Levels 3 & 4* .... Kjos West
Bastien, James .... *Country, Western 'n Blues, Book 2* .... GWM/Kjos
Bastien, Jane S. .... *Pop, Rock 'n Blues, Book 3* .... GWM/Kjos
Brimhall, John .... *Exercises in Rhythm* .... Hansen
Brimhall, John .... *Piano Blues* .... Hansen
Brubeck, Dave .... *Jazz Impressions of New York* .... Marks/Belwin
Brubeck, Dave .... *Themes from Eurasia* .... Shawnee
Clarke, Lucia .... *Jazz and All That!, Sets 1 & 2* .... Myklas
Dennis, Matt .... *Blues Piano Styles* .... Mel Bay
Dennis, Matt .... *Jazz Piano Styles* .... Mel Bay
Dennis, Matt .... *Ragtime Piano Styles* .... Mel Bay
Dennis, Matt .... *Rock Piano Styles* .... Mel Bay
Gillock, William .... *New Orleans Jazz Styles* .... Willis
Gillock, William .... *More New Orleans Jazz Styles* .... Willis
Gillock, William .... *Still More New Orleans Jazz Styles* .... Willis
Gordon, Lewis .... *Introduction to the Art of Rock* .... Belwin
Gordon, Lewis .... *Jazz for Junior* .... Marks/Belwin
Gordon, Lewis .... *Junior Jazz* .... Marks/Belwin
Grove, Roger .... *Jazz About* .... GWM/Kjos
Kasschau, Howard .... *25 Ventures in Rock, Western & Blues* .... Schirmer
King, Stanford .... *I'm Playing Ragtime* .... Fischer
Konowitz, Bert .... *Jazz for Piano, Books 1 & 2* .... Lee Roberts
Konowitz, Bert .... *Jazz is a Way of Playing* .... Lee Roberts
Olson/Bianchi/Blickenstaff ..... *Something Light, Levels 3-5* .... Fischer
Small, Allan (arr.) .... *Ragtime Piano* .... Alfred
Stecher/Horowitz/Gordon ..... *Rock With Jazz, Books 3-5* .... Schirmer
Stecher/Horowitz/Gordon ..... *Rock, Rhythm and Rag, Books 3-5* .... Schirmer
Strommen, Carl .... *Piano a la Jazz* .... Schirmer

Improvisation/Pop Albums...

Intermediate
Adler, Wilfred .... *Piano Improvising* .... Mel Bay
Edison, Roger .... *Learn to Play the Alfred Way: Jazz Piano* .... Alfred
Ferguson, Tom .... *Instant Improvisation at the Piano* .... Alfred
Gutcheon, Jeffrey .... *Improvising Rock Piano* .... Consolidated
Haerle, Dan .... *Jazz Improvisation for Keyboard Players* .... Studio P/R
Keys, Preston .... *Techniques & Theory for Pop Keyboard Players* .... Studio P/R

Konowitz, Bert	The Complete Rock Piano Method	Alfred
Small, Allan	Learn to Play the Alfred Way: Disco Piano	Alfred
Small, Allan	Learn to Play the Alfred Way: Rock Piano	Alfred
Southern, Jeri	Interpreting Popular Music at the Keyboard	Studio P/R

Technic Collections...

Exercise Books (easy-intermediate)...

Aiken, Kenneth	Modern Technic	Willis
Bastien, James (ed.)	First Hanon Studies	Kjos West
Brimhall, John	Hanon Through the Keys	Hansen
Brimhall, John (ed.)	Beringer: Daily Pianoforte Exercises	Hansen
(collection)	Scales, Chords, Arpeggios & Octaves	Shapiro, Bernstein & Co.
Ferte, Armand	The Young Pianist Virtuoso	Schott
Hertz, Henri	Scales and Exercises	Schirmer
Last, Joan	Freedom Technic, Books 1-3	Oxford
Philipp, Isidor	Exercises de Tenues	Marks
Pischna, Johann (Bernard Wolff, ed.)	The Little Pischna	Schirmer

Etude Books (intermediate)...

Bastien, James (ed.)	Czerny and Hanon	GWM/Kjos
Burgmüller, Johann	25 Progressive Pieces, Op. 100	Alfred, Schirmer, others
Czerny, Carl	The School of Velocity, Op. 299	Alfred, Schirmer, Kalmus, others
Germer, Heinrich (ed.)	Czerny: Selected Piano Studies, Vol. 1	Boston Music Co.
Kasschau, Howard (ed.)	106 Greatest Piano Studies, 2 Vols.	Schirmer
Liebling, Emil (ed.)	Selected Czerny Studies, Book 1	Presser
Waxman, Donald	Fifty Etudes, Books 1-4	Galaxy

Duets...

Easy

Bastien, Jane S.	Duet Favorites, Level 3	Kjos West
Bishop, Dorothy	A Folk Holiday	Fischer
George, Jon	Kaleidoscope Duets, Books 2 & 3	Alfred
Johnson, Thomas	You and I	Hinrichsen
Johnson, Thomas	Together We Play	Hinrichsen
Olson/Bianchi/Blickenstaff	Ensemble 3	Fischer
Stecher/Horowitz/Gordon	The Pleasure of Your Company, Books 2 & 3	Fischer

Intermediate

Agay, Denes (arr.)	Joplin-Ragtime Classics	Marks
Bastien, Jane	Duet Favorites, Level 4	Kjos West
Bradley, Richard (arr.)	Bradley's Double Joy	Columbia
Brimhall, John (arr.)	The Rage is Recital Duets	Hansen
Clarke, Lucia	Jazz Duets 1 & 2	Myklas
Dello Joio, Norman	Family Album	Marks
Eckard, Walter (ed.)	44 Original Piano Duets	Presser
George, Jon	Kaleidoscope Duets, Books 4 & 5	Alfred
Marwick and Nagy (arr.)	Folk Song Duets, Level 2	Screen Gems
Metis, Frank	Pop/Rock Sketches for Piano Duet	Marks
Olson/Bianchi/Blickenstaff	Ensemble 4 & 5	Fischer
Stecher/Horowitz/Gordon	The Pleasure of Your Company, Books 4 & 5	Schirmer
Weekley and Arganbright (eds.)	Twice as Nice, Vols. 1-3	Kjos West
Zeitlin and Goldberger (eds.)	The Duet Books, Books 1-3	Consolidated
Zeitlin and Goldberger (eds.)	Easy Piano Duets of the 19th Century	Schroeder & Gunther
Zeitlin and Goldberger (eds.)	Easy Original Piano Duets	Consolidated

Assignments

1st Lesson	5th Lesson
2nd Lesson	6th Lesson
3rd Lesson	7th Lesson
4th Lesson	8th Lesson

9th Lesson	13th Lesson
10th Lesson	14th Lesson
11th Lesson	15th Lesson
12th Lesson	16th Lesson

Index of Music ...

Original Piano Literature

Theme Arrangements

Songs and Folk Songs

Popular Styles

General Index ...